Michael M. Dediu

Three Great Professors:
President Woodrow Wilson
Historian Germán Arciniegas
Mathematician Gheorghe Vrănceanu

A chronological and photographic documentary

DERC Publishing House
Tewksbury (Boston), Massachusetts, U. S. A.

Copyright ©2017 by Michael M. Dediu

All rights reserved

Published and printed in the
United States of America
On the Great Seal of the United States are included:
E Pluribus Unum (Out of many, one)
Annuit Coeptis (He has approved of the undertakings)
Novus Ordo Seclorum (New order of the ages)

Library of Congress Control Number: 2017914445

Dediu, Michael M.

Three great professors: Wilson, Arciniegas, Vranceanu
A chronological and photographic documentary

ISBN-13: 978-1-939757548

1-5829325031
1-2OEMO1Z
03432C
264T9NJ3
1-2OEMO26

Preface

Aristotle (384 BC – 322 BC) said in an aphorism "Everybody, by nature, desires knowledge", therefore great professors, who provide good knowledge in an elegant style, are always remembered. This book is focused on three such great professors: President Wilson, historian Arciniegas, and mathematician Vranceanu, offering, in a chronological order (only this chronological order gives the correct perspective of events and personalities at any given time, because the time determines everything), a variety of relevant information not only about the professors, but also about the numerous important events which took place during their prodigious activities. There are also over 120 attractive and historic photographs (which add another dimension, because they give the possibility to see different places at different times, with different people) that span practical knowledge across multi-length and multi-time scales, with significant details about famous places. The more you read, the more you'll love it! There is also an Addendum for future generations, with very serious items.

This book brings a rainbow of practical information, from the 14th U. S. President Franklin Pierce, to the Prime Minister of France Georges Clemenceau, and to the great Russian writer Aleksandr Solzhenitsyn, and all this information will certainly enhance everybody's joie de vivre.

I want to thank my wife Sophia for her assistance.

These Professors are very important, and any reader, no matter from what part of the world, will definitely find, in this book of general interest, numerous images and useful information, which will help them, as well as future generations, to improve their quality of life.

Michael M. Dediu, Ph. D.

Tewksbury (Boston), U. S. A., 18 September 2017

Three great professors: Wilson, Arciniegas, Vranceanu

Michael M. Dediu is also the author of these books (which can be found on Amazon.com):

1. Aphorisms and quotations – with examples and explanations
2. Axioms, aphorisms and quotations – with examples and explanations
3. 100 Great Personalities and their Quotations
4. Professor Petre P. Teodorescu – A Great Mathematician and Engineer
5. Professor Ioan Goia – A Dedicated Engineering Professor
6. Venice (Venezia) – a new perspective. A short presentation with photographs
7. La Serenissima (Venice) - a new photographic perspective. A short presentation with many photos
8. Grand Canal – Venice. A new photographic viewpoint. A short presentation with many photos
9. Piazza San Marco – Venice. A different photographic view. A short presentation with many photos
10. Roma (Rome) - La Città Eterna. A new photographic view. A short presentation with many photos
11. Why is Rome so Fascinating? A short presentation with many photos
12. Rome, Boston and Helsinki. A short photographic presentation
13. Rome and Tokyo – two captivating cities. A short photographic presentation
14. Beautiful Places on Earth – A new photographic presentation
15. From Niagara Falls to Mount Fuji via Rome - A novel photographic presentation
16. From the USA and Canada to Italy and Japan - A fresh photographic presentation
17. Paris – Why So Many Call This City Mon Amour - A lovely photographic presentation
18. The City of Light – Paris (La Ville-Lumière) - A kaleidoscopic photographic presentation
19. Paris (Lutetia Parisiorum) – the romance capital of the world - A kaleidoscopic photographic view
20. Paris and Tokyo – a joyful photographic presentation. With a preamble about the Universe

21. From USA to Japan via Canada – A cheerful photographic documentary
22. 200 Wonderful Places, In The Last 50 Years – A personal photographic documentary
23. Must see places in USA and Japan - A kaleidoscopic photographic documentary
24. Grandeurs of the World - A kaleidoscopic photographic documentary
25. Corneliu Leu – writer on the same wavelength as Mark Twain. An American viewpoint
26. From Berkeley to Pompeii via Rome – A kaleidoscopic photographic documentary
27. From America to Europe via Japan - A kaleidoscopic photographic documentary
28. Discover America and Japan - A photographic documentary
29. J. R. Lucas – philosopher on a creative parallel with Plato, An American viewpoint
30. From America to Switzerland via France - A photographic documentary
31. From Bretton Woods to New York via Cape Cod - A photographic documentary
32. Splendid Places on the Atlantic Coast of the U. S. A. - A photographic documentary
33. Fourteen nice Cities on three Continents - A photographic documentary
34. 17 Picturesque Cities on the World Map - A photographic documentary
35. Unforgettable Places from Four Continents including Trump buildings - A photographic documentary
36. Dediu Newsletter, Volume 1, Number 1, 6 December 2016 – Monthly news, review, comments and suggestions for a better and wiser world
37. Dediu Newsletter, Volume 1, Number 2, 6 January 2017 (available at www.derc.com).
38. Dediu Newsletter, Volume 1, Number 3, 6 February 2017 (available at www.derc.com).
39. London and Greenwich, A photographic documentary
40. Dediu Newsletter, Volume 1, Number 4, 6 March 2017 (available also at www.derc.com).

41. Dediu Newsletter, Volume 1, Number 5, 6 April 2017 (available also at www.derc.com).
42. Dediu Newsletter, Volume 1, Number 6, 6 May 2017 (available also at www.derc.com).
43. Dediu Newsletter, Volume 1, Number 7, 6 June 2017 (available also at www.derc.com).
44. London, Oxford and Cambridge, A photographic documentary
45. Dediu Newsletter, Volume 1, Number 8, 6 July 2017 (available also at www.derc.com).
46. Dediu Newsletter, Volume 1, Number 9, 6 August 2017 (available also at www.derc.com).
47. Dediu Newsletter, Volume 1, Number 10, 6 September 2017 (available also at www.derc.com).

Michael M. Dediu is the editor of these books (also on Amazon.com):

1. Sophia Dediu: The life and its torrents – Ana. In Europe around 1920
2. Proceedings of the 4th International Conference "Advanced Composite Materials Engineering" COMAT 2012
3. Adolf Shvedchikov: I am an eternal child of spring – poems in English, Italian, French, German, Spanish and Russian
4. Adolf Shvedchikov: Life's Enigma – poems in English, Italian and Russian
5. Adolf Shvedchikov: Everyone wants to be HAPPY – poems in English, Spanish and Russian
6. Adolf Shvedchikov: My Life, My Love – poems in English, Italian and Russian
7. Adolf Shvedchikov: I am the gardener of love – poems in English and Russian
8. Adolf Shvedchikov: Amaretta di Saronno – poems in English and Russian
9. Adolf Shvedchikov: A Russian Rediscovers America
10. Adolf Shvedchikov: Parade of Life - poems in English and Russian
11. Adolf Shvedchikov: Overcoming Sorrow - poems in English and Russian
12. Sophia Dediu: Sophia meets Japan
13. Corneliu Leu: Roosevelt, Churchill, Stalin and Hitler: Their surprising role in Eastern Europe in 1944
14. Proceedings of the 5th International Conference "Computational Mechanics and Virtual Engineering" COMEC 2013
15. Georgeta Simion – Potanga: Beyond Imagination: A Thought-provoking novel inspired from mid-20th century events
16. Ana Dediu: The poetry of my life in Europe and The USA
17. Ana Dediu: The Four Graces
18. Proceedings of the 5th International Conference "Advanced Composite Materials Engineering" COMAT 2014
19. Sophia Dediu: Chocolate Cook Book: Is there such a thing as too much chocolate?

20. Sorin Vlase: Mechanical Identifiability in Automotive Engineering
21. Gabriel Dima: The Evolution of the Aerostructures – Concept and Technologies
22. Proceedings of the 6th International Conference "Computational Mechanics and Virtual Engineering" COMEC 2015
23. Sophia Dediu: Cook Book 1 A-B-C Common sense cooking
24. Sophia Dediu: Dim Sum Spring Festival

Three great professors: Wilson, Arciniegas, Vranceanu

Table of Contents

Preface 3
Table of Contents 11
Chapter 1. Young Wilson 13
Chapter 2. Professor Wilson 20
Chapter 3. Young Vranceanu and Arciniegas 25
Chapter 4. President Wilson 29
Chapter 5. Professor Vranceanu 61
Chapter 6. Professor Arciniegas, Minister 77
Chapter 7. Academician Vranceanu, Ambassador Arciniegas 111
Chapter 8. Other photographs 123
Addendum: For future generations 143

Three great professors: Wilson, Arciniegas, Vranceanu

Chapter 1. Young Wilson

1856. On December 28 Thomas Woodrow Wilson was born in Staunton, Virginia, at 18–24 North Coalter Street, to a Scots-Irish American family. He was the third of four children of Joseph Ruggles Wilson (1822–1903) and Jessie Janet Woodrow (1826–1888). His childhood home is now the Woodrow Wilson Presidential Library.

The 14th U. S. President at that time was Franklin Pierce: 1853-1857, 1804-1869 (64), before he was Brigadier General

Washington: Woodrow Wilson International Center for Scholars (1968). There is now the 1913 Centennial, in celebration of the 100th anniversary of President Woodrow Wilson's inauguration.

1857. The 15th U. S. President was James Buchanan: 1857-1861, 1791-1868 (77), U. S. Minister to the Court of St. James's, UK (which is the royal court for the Sovereign of the United Kingdom (Victoria (1819-1901 (81), Queen 1837-1901, had 9 children), named after St. James's Palace, but the title of the Court is transferred to the location where the Sovereign currently resides),

1861. April 12 – American Civil War starts. Wilson's father was one of the founders of the Southern Presbyterian Church in the United States (PCUS).

The 16th U. S. President was Abraham Lincoln: 1861-1865, 1809-1865 (56), U.S. Representative from Illinois' 7th District.

1865. May 9 – American Civil War ends by proclamation.

The 17th U. S. President was Andrew Johnson: 1865-1869, 1808-1875 (66), before he was the 16th Vice President of the U. S.

Mark Twain is 30 years old, and, after moving to San Francisco, writes "Jim Smiley and His Jumping Frog".

UK King George V was born (1865 – 1936, King 1910 – 1936, had 6 children).

Shakespeare's quote: *Love all, trust a few, do wrong to none.*

USA, Cleveland, April 1979, Case Western Reserve University (1826), Yost Hall, the private doctorate-granting university was created in 1967 by the federation of Case Institute of Technology (1881 by Leonard Case Jr. (1820-1880)) and Western Reserve University (1826), acceptance rate 36%, 7 km east of downtown, undergraduates 5,100, postgraduates 6,200, 63 ha campus, 16 Nobel

1866. Because of the turmoil of the Civil War, Woodrow's education was inconsistent. It is also said that he had dyslexia, and he didn't learn to read until he was ten years old.

Mark Twain 31, takes a trip to Hawaii, as correspondent of the Sacramento newspaper "Alta California", and gives his first public lecture. Next year he travels as correspondent to Europe and the Holy Land, sees a picture of Olivia Langdon (Livy), and publishes "The Celebrated Jumping Frog of Calaveras County, and Other Sketches".

1869. The 18th U. S. President was Ulysses S. Grant: 1869-1877, 1822-1885 (63), Commanding General of the U.S. Army.

Twain, 34, after many lectures across the U.S., meets and is engaged to Livy. He publishes "The Innocents Abroad", as a subscription book, and it is an instant best seller.

1870. Wilson's father became minister of the First Presbyterian Church in Augusta, Georgia, and the family lived there until 1870, when young Wilson was 14. Wilson lived in Columbia, South Carolina, from 1870 to 1874, while his father was professor at the Columbia Theological Seminary.

1873 At 17 Wilson became a communicant member of the Columbia First Presbyterian Church in South Carolina, and remained a member throughout his life. Wilson attended Davidson College (established 1837, motto: Alenda Lux Ubi Orta Libertas (Let Learning Be Cherished Where Liberty Has Arisen), faculty 170, undergraduates 1.950 on campus) in North Carolina for the 1873–74 school year, cut short by illness, then transferred to Princeton University (established 1746, motto Dei Sub Numine Viget (Under God's Power He Flourishes), faculty 1,238, students 8,200) as a freshman.

Twain, 38, invents and patents "Mark Twain's Self-Pasting Scrapboo", and publishes "The Gilded Age".

Belgium, 19 March 1978, Bruxelles (990, population 1.1 M), from Grand Place looking southeast to the northwest façades of Guildhalls, 1698, Maison des Brasseurs with Beer museum (center).

USA, Cleveland, 9 August 1979, The Fountain of Eternal Life, in front of the old Cleveland Board of Education building (1931-2013, the author worked here 1980-1985, from 2016 Drury Plaza Hotel).

1874 His father moved the family to Wilmington, North Carolina, where he was the minister at First Presbyterian Church until 1882.

1877 The 19th U. S. President was Rutherford B. Hayes: 1877-1881, 1822-1893 (70), 29th & 32nd Governor of Ohio.
Twain published the previous year, 1876, "Tom Sawyer".

1879 At 23, Woodrow graduated, a member of Phi Kappa Psi fraternity, at Princeton University, where he studied philosophy and history. Wilson attended law school at the University of Virginia (founded by Thomas Jefferson (Founding Father, principal author of the Declaration of Independence, and the third President of the United States from 1801 to 1809, 1743-1826 (83)) in 1819, James Madison (Founding Father, the fourth President of the United States from 1809 to 1817, 1751-1836 (85)) was the 2nd rector, until 1836, faculty 2100, students 22,400) for one year.

1881 The 20th U. S. President was James A. Garfield: March 4 – Sep 19, 1881 (6.5 months), 1831-1881 (49), U.S. Representative for Ohio's 19th District.
The 21st U. S. President was Chester A. Arthur: 1881-1885, 1829-1886 (57), before he was the 20th Vice President of the U. S.

1883 Wilson entered Johns Hopkins University (private research university in Baltimore, Maryland, founded in 1876, named for its first benefactor, the American entrepreneur, and philanthropist Johns Hopkins (1795-1873 (78))) to study history, political philosophy and the German language. He met and fell in love with Ellen Louise Axson, the daughter of a minister from Savannah, Georgia; he proposed to her, and they became engaged in Asheville.
Twain, 48, after two years ago (1881) published "Prince and the Pauper", publishes "Life on the Mississippi".

USA, Michigan, west Detroit area, May 1979, Dearborn: a nice building with statues.

USA, Michigan, Detroit, May 1979, the first factory of the Ford Motor Company, Mack Avenue 1903 plant, 5 km north of Canada.

Chapter 2. Professor Wilson

1885 At 29, Woodrow married Ellen Axson. They had three daughters. Wilson published his first book "Congressional Government". He completed his doctoral dissertation, *Congressional Government: A Study in American Politics*, and received a Ph.D. He taught at Bryn Mawr College (1885, in Bryn Mawr, Pennsylvania) from 1885 until 1888, teaching ancient Greek and Roman history.

The 22nd U. S. President was Grover Cleveland: 1885-1889, 1837-1908 (71), 28th Governor of New York.

Twain published the year before (1884) in London "The Adventures of Huckleberry Finn", and this year the American edition comes out. Clemens (Mark Twain) turns 50, publishes the memoirs of Ulysses S. Grant (1822 – 1885, the 18th U.S. President (1869 – 1877)), memoirs now considered a literary classic.

Socrates' quote: *True wisdom comes to each of us when we comprehend how little we understand about life, ourselves, and the world around us.*

1886 Wilson, 30, worked as a lecturer at Cornell University (1865, by Ezra Cornell (1807-1874 (67), businessman and politician, on his farm in Ithaca, New York), faculty 2,900 in Ithaca, New York City and Doha (Qatar), 22,000 students) in 1886–1887. Their first daughter, Margaret, was born on April 16, 1886 (died Feb 12, 1944 (57) in India).

USA, July 1980, New York Harbor, Statue of Liberty (1886, 93 m) on Liberty Island, with grandmother (left) and grandson (right).

1887 Their second daughter, Jessie, was born on August 28, 1887 (died Jan 15, 1933 (45) in Cambridge, Massachusetts).

1888 Wilson, 32, left Bryn Mawr for Wesleyan University (1831 in Middletown, Connecticut), where was inducted into Phi Beta Kappa, and founded the debate team, which bears his name. His mother died at 62.

USA, Michigan, Detroit, Dearborn, May 1979, The Henry Ford Museum (1929), with some of the first Ford cars.

USA, Michigan, Detroit, Dearborn, May 1979, an old wind mill

1889 Their third daughter, Eleanor, was born on October 16, 1889 (died on April 5, 1967 (77) in Montecito, California).

The 23rd U. S. President was Benjamin Harrison: 1889-1893, 1833-1901 (67), U.S. Senator from Indiana.

1890 In February 1890, with the help of friends, Wilson, 34, was elected by the Princeton University board to the Chair of Jurisprudence and Political Economy, at an annual salary of $3,000. Additionally, Wilson became the first lecturer of Constitutional Law at New York Law School (1891 in Tribeca, Lower Manhattan, New York City).

Twain, 55, after publishing, one year ago (1889), "A Connecticut Yankee in King Arthur's Court", (King Arthur was a legendary British king, circa 470 – 530), which was extensively criticized, buys all rights in the Paige typesetter. His mother Jane, 87, passes in eternity.

1893 The 24th U. S. President was Grover Cleveland: 1893-1897, 1837-1908 (71), 22nd Vice President of the United States.

1896 Wilson published his second book "George Washington".

Twain, two years ago (1894), after he leaves Hartford, in 1891, to live in Europe, because of financial problems, publishes "Pudd'nhead Wilson", his publishing company fails, and he files for bankruptcy.

Twain, now 61, continues for a second year to lecture around the world, to restore his finances, but his daughter Susy, 24, passes to eternity.

1897 Wilson published his third book "On Being Human".

The 25th U. S. President was William McKinley: 1897-1901, 1843-1901 (58), 39th Governor of Ohio.

1898 Wilson published his forth book "The State: Elements of Historical and Practical Politics".

Italy, 12 May 1978, Bologna (1000 BC, 140 km², elevation 54 m, metro population 1 M, the capital and largest city of the Emilia-Romagna region in Northern Italy, with the oldest university in the world, University of Bologna, founded in 1088), west of Piazza di Porta San Donato, from Via Zamboni looking east to the north façade of the Università degli studi di Bologna, Dipartimento di Matematica, Istituto di Matematica.

Chapter 3. Young Vranceanu and Arciniegas

1900 On June 30, in Valea Hogei, Lipova, Bacău County, Romania, Gheorghe Vrănceanu was born in a farmer family.

On December 6, in Bogotá, Colombia, the son of Rafael Arciniegas Tavera, a farmer, and his wife Aurora Angueyra Figueredo, was born: Germán Arciniegas. He had three brothers and four sisters. His father died young, leaving his mother struggling to support the family. His maternal great-grandfather was Perucho Figueredo, an early Cuban freedom fighter, who wrote La Bayamesa, Cuba's national anthem. Both of Perucho's daughters fled the country when he was executed. Luz, the younger daughter, was married to a Cuban engineer, who went to Colombia to help build a railroad line. It was there, in the jungle, that Germán's mother was born.

1901 The 26th U. S. President was Theodore Roosevelt: 1901-1909, 1858-1919 (60), 25th Vice President of the U.S.

1902 The Princeton trustees promoted Professor Wilson, 46, to president in June 1902. He published his fifth book "A History of the American People" in 5 volumes.

1903 His father died at 81.

1906 Wilson, 50, awoke one day to find himself blind in the left eye, the result of a blood clot and hypertension. Modern medical opinion surmises Wilson had suffered a stroke—he later was diagnosed, as his father had been, with hardening of the arteries.
Twain, two years ago (1904), after finishing to pay off all the creditors (even if he was protected by bankruptcy), suffers the loss of his beloved wife for 34 years, Livy, 59. He begins dictating autobiography, and moves to New York City.
Twain, one year ago (1905), at 70, is the guest of Theodore Roosevelt (1858 – 1919, the 26th U.S. President (1901 – 1909)) at the White House, has a banquet for his 70th birthday in New York, speaks frequently, and addresses congressional committee on copyright issues.

Italy, 8 Sep 1977, Cortona (circa 1500 BC, 343 km², elevation 494 m, population 23,000, between Firenze to northwest and Rome to southwest), Il Palazzone, Villa Principesca sec. XVI (1521-1527, by Cardinal Silvio Passerini (1469-1529), Bishop of Cortona), with a tower (42 m, can see Lake Trasimeno 12 km southeast), donated to Scuola Normale Superiore (1810 by Napoleon Bonaparte (1769-1821) di Pisa in 1968 by Count Lorenzo Passerini di Cortona.

1908 Wilson published his sixth book "Constitutional Government in the United States".

1909 Wilson's final year as President of Princeton.

The 27th U. S. President was William Howard Taft: 1909-1913, 1857-1930 (72), 42nd U.S. Secretary of War

Twain, 74, after last year he moved into the Italian style splendid mansion Stormfield in Redding, Connecticut, where he formed the "Angelfish Club" for young girls, suffers the loss of his youngest daughter Jean, 29.

1910 On September 14 Wilson, 54, was nominated for Governor of New Jersey. He submitted his letter of resignation to Princeton on October 20.
Mark Twain, 75, visits Bermuda for the last time, and passes in eternity, of a heart attack, on April 21, in his house at Stormfield. He was buried in his wife's plot at Woodlawn Cemetery in Elmira, New York. His only surviving daughter, Clara, placed a monument there. Mark Twain is considered the father of the American literature.

1911 Wilson ran for Governor of New Jersey, and won the vote by a wide margin.

1912 Wilson decided to run for president. Because he had grown so respected and popular, and because the Republican Party split, he won an easy victory.

USA, Ohio, Cleveland, August 1979, NASA John H. Glenn Research Center (1942, near the airport), Agena rochet (1959-1987).

USA, Ohio, Cleveland, August 1979, NASA John H. Glenn Research Center (1942), Centaur rochet (1962-present, 12.7 m, 3 m)

Chapter 4. President Wilson

1913 Wilson, 57, was sworn as the 28th President of the United States on March 4, 1913. He was the first Southerner elected to the presidency since 1848. He also was the only Democrat, besides Grover Cleveland, to be elected president since 1856. He became the first president to deliver the State of the Union address in person since 1801, as Thomas Jefferson had discontinued this practice. The first press conference was on March 15, 1913, when reporters were allowed to ask him questions. A new federal income tax was introduced, authorized by the 16th Amendment. The Federal Reserve Act passed in December 1913. He's first term as president was marked with hardship. Wilson frequently intervened in Latin American affairs, saying in 1913: "I am going to teach the South American republics to elect good men". Wilson negotiated a treaty with Colombia, in which the U.S. apologized for its role in the Panama Revolution of 1903–1904. Wilson published his seventh book "The New Freedom".

1914 The Federal Trade Commission Act was signed in September 1914. Wilsonian idealism became a reason for American intervention in Latin America until the 1920s and 1930s, when moralistic interventions were abandoned in favor of realism. On August 6, his wife Ellen died at 54, on kidney failure. The Smith–Lever Act of 1914 created the modern system of agricultural extension agents, sponsored by the state agricultural colleges. The agents taught new techniques to farmers.

The elementary teacher noticed the mathematical talent of Gheorghe Vrănceanu, 14, and insisted to the parents to send him to the high school in Vaslui.

Netherlands, 14 August 1977, Amsterdam, in the North See harbor two big ships: Lübeck Linie (center), Naaskerk Antwerpen (right).

Italy, 8 Sep 1977, Cortona (circa 1500 BC, 343 km^2, elevation 494 m, population 23,000), the southwest façade and entrance of Il Palazzone di Cortona (1521-1527, 2 km southeast of Cortona).

On July 28 the World War I started in Europe. Austria-Hungary declares war on Serbia.

August 1st: Germany declares war on Russia. Germany and the Ottoman Empire sign a secret alliance treaty.

August 2nd: Germany invades Luxembourg.

August 3rd: Germany declares war on France.

August 4th: Germany invades Belgium. The United Kingdom declares war on Germany. The United States declares neutrality.

August 5th: Montenegro declares war on Austria-Hungary. The Ottoman Empire closes the Dardanelles.

August 6th: Austria-Hungary declares war on Russia. Serbia declares war on Germany.

August 7th: The British Expeditionary Force arrives in France. Battle of the Frontiers starts, ends Sep. 13. The Germans obtain a victory against the British Expeditionary Force and France's Fifth Army.

August 8th: Montenegro declares war on Germany.

August 11: France declares war on Austria-Hungary.

August 12: The United Kingdom declares war on Austria-Hungary.

August 16-20: The Serbs defeat the Austro-Hungarians at the Battle of Cer.

August 17: The Russian army enters East Prussia. Battle of Stalluponen.

August 20: The Germans occupy Brussels.

August 23: Japan declares war on Germany.

August 25: Japan declares war on Austria-Hungary.

August 28: Austria-Hungary declares war on Belgium.

August 30: New Zealand occupies German Samoa (later Western Samoa).

September 5-12: First Battle of the Marne. The German advance on Paris is halted, marking the failure of the Schlieffen Plan.

September 11: Australian forces occupy German New Guinea.

USA, 23 Jan 2005, near Boston, heavy snow.

Netherlands, 14 Aug 1977, Amsterdam (1275, population 1.3 M, elevation minus 2 m (2 m under the Atlantic Ocean level)): Zijkanaal G, with a bridge for the street s150, and Havenstraat on the left.

September 13: Troops from South Africa begin invading German South-West Africa.

September 28 – Oct 10: The Germans besiege and capture Antwerp, Belgium.

October 29: The Ottoman Empire launches a surprise attack on the Russian Black Sea coast.

November 1: Russia declares war on the Ottoman Empire.

November 2: The United Kingdom begins the naval blockade of Germany.

November 3: Montenegro declares war on the Ottoman Empire.

November 5: France and the United Kingdom declare war on the Ottoman Empire.

November 11: Sultan Mehmed V of the Otoman Empire declares Jihad on the Allies.

1915 Wilson, 59, and Edith Bolling, 43, (1872-1961), southern widow and jeweler, married on December 18, 1915. Wilson was the third president to marry while in office; after John Tyler in 1844 and Grover Cleveland in 1886. Wilson published his eighth and last book "When A Man Comes To Himself".

January 19: First German Zeppelin raid on Great Britain.

January 31: Battle of Bolimov (Poland). First German use of chemical weapons against Russia.

February 4: Germany begins unrestricted submarine warfare against merchant vessels.

April 22 – May 25: The Second Battle of Ypres (western Belgium), which ends in a stalemate. Germany first uses the poison gas.

April 26: Treaty of London – secret pact to gain alliance of Italy with UK, France and Russia.

May 7: The British liner *Lusitania* is sunk by a German U-boat.

May 12: Windhoek, capital of German South-West Africa, is occupied by South African troops.

May 23: Italy declares war on Austria-Hungary.

Italy, 8 Sep 1977, from the road to Il Palazzone (right) di Cortona looking northwest to Cortona (1500 BC, 343 km², elevation 494 m).

Germany, 16 August 1977, Dortmund, Willkommen in Dortmund, the south façade of the Hauptbahnhof (Railway Station).

July 9: The German forces in South-West Africa surrender.
August 5: The Germans occupy Warsaw, Poland.
September 1: Germany suspends unrestricted submarine warfare.
September 8: Tsar Nicholas II of Russia removes Grand Duke Nicholas Nikolayevich as Commander-in-Chief of the Russian Army, and personally takes that position.
September 19: The Germans occupy Vilnius (Lithuania). The Gorlice-Tarnów Offensive ends.
October 7 – Dec 4: Serbia is invaded by Germany, Austria-Hungary, and Bulgaria.
October 14: Bulgaria declares war on Serbia.
October 15: The United Kingdom declares war on Bulgaria.
October 16: France declares war on Bulgaria.
October 19: Italy and Russia declare war on Bulgaria.
October 27: A French army lands in Salonika (Greece) and, with the help of British and Italian troops, sets up a Balkan Front.
October 29: René Viviani resigns as Prime Minister of France; he is replaced by Aristide Briand.
November 27: The Serbian army collapses. It will retreat to the Adriatic Sea, and be evacuated by the Italian and French Navies.

Shakespeare's quote: *Brevity is the soul of wit.*

1916 The 1916 Federal Farm Loan Act provided for issuance of low-cost long-term mortgages to farmers. In spite of the turmoil marking his first term, Americans rallied around Wilson, because he was able to keep them out of the War. The vote was so close that it required a re-count, but Wilson came out the winner.

Germán Arciniegas, 16, created the journal: *Año Quinto.*

January 5-17: Austro-Hungarian offensive against Montenegro, which capitulates.
January 9: The Gallipoli (Dardanelles strait) Campaign ends in an Allied defeat and an Ottoman victory.
January 11: Corfu (Greek island) is occupied by the Allies.

14 Aug 1977, Amsterdam (1275, population 1.3 M, elevation minus 2 m (2 m under the Atlantic Ocean)): the east façade of the Royal Palace (1655 (initially Town Hall, inspired by Roman palaces, first king Louis Napoleon (1778-1846, King of Holland 1806-1810, a younger brother of Napoleon)) built on 13,659 wooden piles (like in Venezia), floor area 22,031 m², with yellowish sandstone from Bentheim in Germany), on the west side of Dam Square.

January 27: Conscription is introduced in the United Kingdom by the Military Service Act 1916.

February 28: German Kamerun (Cameroon) surrenders.

March 1: Germany resumes unrestricted submarine warfare.

March 9: Germany declares war on Portugal. Portugal officially enters the war.

May 10: Germany suspends unrestricted submarine warfare.

May 16: Signing of the Sykes-Picot Agreement between Britain and France, defining their proposed spheres of influence in the Middle East.

June 10: Italy: Paolo Boselli succeeds Antonio Salandra as Prime Minister.

July 1-3: The Social Democratic Party wins a majority in the parliament of the Russian-ruled Grand Duchy of Finland.

August 27: Romania enters the war on the Entente's (UK, France, Russia) side.

August 27 – December: Conquest of part of Romania by Central Powers (Germany, Austro-Hungary, Ottoman Empire, Bulgaria).

August 28: Italy declares war on Germany.

September 15-22: Battle of Flers-Courcelette (France); the British use armored tanks for the first time in history.

November 21: Francis Joseph I, Emperor of Austria and King of Hungary, dies and is succeeded by Charles I.

December 5-7: United Kingdom: Prime Minister H. H. Asquith resigns and is succeeded by David Lloyd George.

December 6: The Germans occupy Bucharest. The capital of Romania moved to Iași.

December 18: Battle of Verdun (sur Meuse, France, for almost 10 months) ends with French victory, and enormous casualties on both sides.

Netherlands, 14 Aug 1977, Amsterdam (1275, population 1.3 M, elevation minus 2 m (2 m under the Atlantic Ocean level)), near a petit restaurant on Rozenboomsteeg, near the Amsterdam Museum (1926, a museum about the history of Amsterdam) and Universiteitsbibliotheek Singel (the library of the University of Amsterdam and the Academic Medical Center, is in the town center at Singel, close to Heiligeweg and Koningsplein).

1917 In January, Germany's foreign minister sent Mexico the Zimmermann Telegram, inviting it to join in war against the United States. In March 1917 several American ships were sunk by Germany, then the cabinet was unanimously in favor of war. In spite of the Americans' wish to stay out of the war, President Wilson recognized that not stepping in to fight could result in an end to their way of life. He declared war on April 2, 1917. The declaration of war by the United States against Germany passed Congress by strong bipartisan majorities on April 4, 1917. Wilson refused to make a formal alliance with Britain or France, but operated as an "associated" power—an informal ally with military cooperation through the Supreme War Council in London. The U.S. raised a massive army through conscription, and Wilson gave command to Pershing, with complete authority as to tactics, strategy and some diplomacy. Colonel House was Wilson's main channel of communication with the British government. Future President Herbert Hoover led the Food Administration. March 1917 also brought the first of two revolutions in Russia, which impacted the strategic role of the U.S. in the war. The overthrow of the Russian imperial government removed a serious barrier to America's entry into the European conflict, while the second Russian revolution in November relieved the Germans of a major threat on their eastern front, and allowed them to dedicate more troops to the Western front, thus making U.S. forces central to Allied success in battles of 1918. Wilson initially rebuffed pleas from the Allies to dedicate military resources to an intervention in Russia against the Bolsheviks, based partially on his experience from attempted intervention in Mexico; nevertheless he ultimately was convinced of the potential benefit, and agreed to dispatch a limited force to assist the Allies on the eastern front. After Russia left World War I following the Bolshevik Revolution of 1917, the Allies sent troops there to prevent a German or Bolshevik takeover of allied-provided weapons, munitions and other supplies previously shipped as aid to the pre-revolutionary government. Wilson sent armed forces to assist the withdrawal of Czechoslovak Legions along the Trans-Siberian Railway, and to hold key port cities at Arkhangelsk and Vladivostok.

Japan, Nov. 1993, Osaka: the north side of the Osaka Castle (1597, 58 m, by Toyotomi Hideyoshi, rebuilt, with a museum), 5 km southeast of Shin-Osaka Station, with the entrance to the Osaka Castle, after Yamaguchimon Gate.

Though specifically instructed not to engage the Bolsheviks, the U.S. forces engaged in several armed conflicts against forces of the new Russian government. Revolutionaries in Russia resented the United States intrusion. Wilson withdrew most of the soldiers on April 1, 1920, though some remained until as late as 1922. The Germans launched an offensive at Arras.

Germán Arciniegas, 17, created the journal *Voz de la Juventud*.

January 9: Battle of Rafa (on the Sinai-Palestine border). The British drive the Ottomans out of Sinai.
January 16: The German Foreign Secretary Arthur Zimmermann sends a telegram to his ambassador in Mexico, instructing him to propose to the Mexican government an alliance against the United States.
February 1: Germany resumes unrestricted submarine warfare.
March 8-11: The British capture Baghdad, Iraq.
March 15: Russia: Czar Nicholas II abdicates. A provisional government is appointed.
March 17: Aristide Briand resigns as Prime Minister of France; he is replaced by Alexandre Ribot.
April 6: The United States declares war on Germany.
May 15: Philippe Pétain replaces Robert Nivelle as Commander-in-Chief of the French Army.
June 12: Greece: King Constantine I abdicates.
June 13: First successful heavy bomber raid on London done by the German Gotha G.IV.
June 25: First American troops land in France.
June 27: Batterie Pommern ('Lange Max', 38 cm), world's largest gun, fires for the first time from Koekelare (Belgium) to Dunkirk (northern France, 50 km from Koekelare).
June 30: Greece declares war on the Central powers (Germany, etc.).
July 1-19: The Russian Kerensky Offensive fails. It is the last Russian initiative in the war.

1 Oct 1977, Milano, in Piazza del Duomo, part of the façade of il Duomo (Basilica cattedrale metropolitana di Santa Maria Nascente, 1386-1965 (579 years), capacity 40,000, length 158.5 m, width 92 m, maximum height 108 m, 135 spires, materials: brick and Candoglia marble, architects: Donato Bramante (1444-1514), Leonardo da Vinci (1452-1519), Giulio Romano (1499-1546), Pellegrino Tibaldi (1527-1596)). On May 20, 1805, Napoleon Bonaparte (1769-1821), about to be crowned King of Italy, ordered the façade to be finished by Pellicani. For this, a statue of Napoleon was placed at the top of one of the spires. Napoleon was crowned King of Italy at the Duomo on May 26, 1805.

July 6: Arab rebels led by Lawrence of Arabia seize the Jordanian port of Aqaba.

July 20: Corfu Declaration about the future Kingdom of Yugoslavia.

July 21: Alexander Kerensky replaces Georgy Lvov as Minister-President of the Russian Provisional Government.

August 6-20: Battle of Mărășești, Romania – troops from Romania and Russian Republic succsessfuly defend the northeastern region of Romania (called Moldova) against Germany and Austro-Hungary.

September 8: Russia: General Kornilov's coup attempt fails.

September 12: Alexandre Ribot resigns as Prime Minister of France; he is replaced by Paul Painlevé.

October 30: Italy: Vittorio Emanuele Orlando succeeds Paolo Boselli as Prime Minister.

November 5: The Allies agree to establish a Supreme War Council at Versailles.

November 7: The October Revolution begins in Russia. The Bolsheviks seize power.

November 13: France: Paul Painlevé is replaced by Georges Clemenceau as Prime Minister.

November 17-30: Battle of Jerusalem. The British enter the city (December 11).

November 25: Battle of Ngomano (now in Mozambique), the Germans invade Portuguese East Africa to gain supplies.

December 7: The United States declares war on Austria-Hungary.

December 16: Russia signs a preliminary armistice with Germany.

27 April 1978, a statue in Fribourg (started at the beginning of the Roman era (27 BC – 1453), founded in 1157 by Berchtold IV von Zähringen (1125-1186), western Switzerland, elevation 531 m (La Sarine river) to 702 m, population 38,000, area 9.3 km^2, on both sides of the river Sarine, on the Swiss Plateau, on the border between German and French Switzerland, the best-maintained Old City sits on a small rocky hill above the valley of the Sarine).

1918 A speech by Wilson to Congress on January 8, 1918, articulated America's long term war objectives. It was the clearest expression of intention made by any of the belligerent nations. The speech was known as the Fourteen Points. The German offensive prompted an accelerated deployment of troops by Wilson to the Western front—by August 1918 a million American troops had reached France. The Allies initiated a counter offensive at Somme, and by August the Germans had lost the military initiative, and an Allied victory was in sight. In October came a message from the new German Chancellor Prince Max of Baden to Wilson, requesting a general armistice. In the exchange of notes with Germany they agreed the Fourteen Points in principle be incorporated in the armistice. Colonel House then procured agreement from France and Britain, but only after threatening to conclude a unilateral armistice without them. Wilson ignored Gen. Pershing's plea to drop the armistice, and instead demand an unconditional surrender by Germany. On November 11, 1918, the World War I ends. With congressional elections in the US approaching, in 1918 Wilson made an appeal to the public for the retention of a Democratic majority, and this seriously backfired, due to its self-serving tone – Republicans successfully picked up majorities in both houses of Congress. Wilson spent six months in Paris for the Peace Conference, thereby becoming the first U.S. president to travel to Europe while in office. He disembarked from the *George Washington* in Brest on December 13, 1918.

Germán Arciniegas, 18, began studying law at the National University of Colombia.

On December 11, Aleksandr Solzhenitsyn was born in Kislovodsk, Russia (200 km east of the Black Sea, 300 km west of the Caspian Sea, 600 km southwest of Volgograd). His father died six months before his birth.

February to September: Allied forces occupy the Jordan Rift Valley (all around Jordan River).

23 March 1978, the Historical Merchants' Hall of 1520-1530, façade decorated with statues and the coat of arms of four Habsburg (1027-1780) emperors, in Freibourg im Breisgau (1120 by Duke Berthold III of Zähringen (1085-1122), elevation 278 m, population 222,000, area 153 km^2), southwest Germany, near France and Switzerland.

February 9: The Central Powers (Germany, etc.) signed an exclusive protectorate treaty with the Ukrainian People's Republic (existed only 3 years, 1918 - 1921), as part of the negotiations that took place in Brest-Litovsk (in German occupied Ukraine, now in Belarus at the border with Poland).

February 21: The British capture Jericho (in the West Bank near the Jordan River).

Germans capture Minsk (capital of Belarus).

February 25: German troops capture Estonia.

March 2: Germans capture Kiev (capital of Ukraine).

March 3: At Brest-Litovsk, Russian Leon Trotsky signs the peace treaty with Germany.

March 7: German artillery bombard the Americans at Rouge Bouquet (near the French village of Baccarat), killing 19.

March 23 –August 7: German artillery bombardment of Paris.

March 26: French Marshal Ferdinand Foch is appointed Supreme Commander of all Allied forces.

April 1: UK Royal Air Force founded by combining the Royal Flying Corps and the Royal Naval Air Service.

May 7: Treaty of Bucharest between Romania and the Central Powers. It will never be ratified.

May 21: Ottomans invade Armenia.

June 8 – October: Germany interferes in the Caucasus.

June 8: total Solar eclipse in the U. S., from the southwest corner of Washington state, passed over Denver, Jackson (Mississippi) and Orlando before exiting the country at the Atlantic coast of Florida.

June 13-23: Second Battle of the Piave: the Austro-Hungarian offensive is repelled.

July 15 0 August 6: Second Battle of the Marne and last German offensive on the Western Front, which fails when the Germans are counterattacked by the French.

July 17: The Russian Tsar and his family were shot early in the morning by the Bolsheviks.

20 May 1978, on the main square Place de la Réunion, looking east to the southwest façade of L'église Saint-Étienne (called Cathédrale, 1866, 97 m bell tower) de Mulhouse (1150, elevation 232-338 m, population 112,000, area 22.18 km², 20 km west of Rhine River (border France and Germany),40 km north of Switzerland, 1354-1515 Free Imperial City, 1515 associated with Swiss Confederation, 1798 France, 1871-1918 Germany), Alsace, east of France.

August 8 – November 11: Hundred Days Offensive (by France, UK, USA, Belgium, Portugal against Germany), last offensive on Western Front. The Allies break through the German lines.

August 26 – September 14: Battle of Baku, last Turkish offensive of the war.

September 14-29: Vardar (Macedonia) Offensive, final offensive on the Balkan Front. The Allies (French and Serbs) break through the Bulgarian lines.

September 19-25: Battle of Megiddo (Ottoman Syria). The British conquer Palestine.

September 26 – October 1: The British enter Damascus (Syria).

September 30: Bulgaria signs an armistice with the Allies.

October 3: Tsar Ferdinand I of Bulgaria abdicates and Boris III accedes to the throne.

October 20: Germany suspends submarine warfare.

October 24 – November 4: Battle of Vittorio Veneto (Italy). The Austro-Hungarian army is routed. The Italians enter Trent and land at Trieste.

October 29: State of Slovenes, Croats and Serbs proclaimed.

October 30: The Ottoman Empire signs the Armistice of Mudros on board HMS *Agamemnon* in Moudros harbor on the Greek island of Lemnos.

October 31: The Hungarian government terminates its union with Austria, officially dissolving the Austro-Hungarian state.

November 3: Austria-Hungary signs the armistice with Italy, effective November 4.

November 6-11: Allied troops advance to the Meuse (a major European river, from France, through Belgium, the Netherlands, draining into the North Sea). The Meuse-Argonne Offensive was the largest in United States military history, involving 1.2 million American soldiers, and was one of a series of Allied attacks known as the Hundred Days Offensive, which brought the war to an end. The battle cost 28,000 German lives and 26,277 American lives, making it the largest and bloodiest operation of World War I for the American Expeditionary Force (AEF), which was commanded by General John J. Pershing, and the deadliest battle in American history.

16 May 1978, Canal du Rhône au Rhin, Mulhouse (1150), France.

18 May 1978, Station de ski du Schnepfenried, France, 3 km southwest of Sondernach, 50 km west of Rhine, France, Le Chalet Amis de la Nature, elevation 1,050 m in the Vosgien Mountain

November 9: Germany: Kaiser William II abdicates; republic proclaimed.

November 10: Austria-Hungary: Kaiser Charles I abdicates.

November 11: At 6 AM, Germany signs the Armistice of Compiègne (a commune in the Oise department in northern France, located on the Oise River). End of fighting at 11 AM.

Poland proclaimed.

November 12: Austria proclaimed a republic.

November 14: Czechoslovakia proclaimed a republic.

German U-boats interned.

Fighting ends in the East African theater when General von Lettow-Vorbeck agrees to a cease-fire, on hearing of Germany's surrender.

November 22: The Germans evacuate Luxembourg.

November 27: The Germans evacuate Belgium.

December 1: Kingdom of Serbs, Croats and Slovenes proclaimed.

In Alba Iulia, The National Assembly of Romanians in Transylvania declares union with the Kingdom of Romania.

1919   While in Italy (January 1–6, 1919) for meetings with King Victor Emmanuel III and Prime Minister Vittorio Orlando, he became the first incumbent U.S. president to have an audience with a reigning pope, when he visited Pope Benedict XV at the Apostolic Palace. In March Wilson suffered an illness, and the ensuing months brought a decline in health and in power and prestige. President Wilson signed the Treaty of Versailles. The President also proposed the League of Nations, which caused fighting in the US. For his peace-making efforts, Wilson was awarded the 1919 Nobel Peace Prize. Wilson had a series of debilitating strokes on September 25 - he collapsed and never fully recovered. On October 2 he suffered a serious stroke, leaving him paralyzed on his left side, along with blindness in his left eye, and with only partial vision in the right eye. He was confined to bed for several weeks, and sequestered from everyone except his wife and physician, Dr. Cary Grayson. For some months, Wilson used a wheelchair and later he required use of a cane. He became an invalid in the White House, closely monitored by his wife, who insulated him from negative news, and downplayed for him the gravity of his condition.

Italy, 18 Nov 1977, Roma, Vatican, Basilica Papale di San Pietro (started 1506, opened 1626, 132 m).

9 Dec 1977, Venezia, with the announcement "Il Dissenso Culturale 15 Nov – 15 Dicembre 1977", on Ponte degli Scalzi.

Gheorghe Vrănceanu is excellent in mathematics, and his mathematics teacher Nicolae Abramescu obtains a Adamachi scholarship for him at the Faculty of Sciences of the University of Iasi. He enrolls at the Section of Mathematics, and has as professors Alexandru Myller, Simion Sanielevici, Victor Valcovici, and Simion Stoilow, who appreciate his mathematical talent.

January 18: Treaty of Versailles between the Allies and Germany: the Peace Conference opens in Paris.
January 18: Proposal to create the League of Nations accepted.
June 21: German High Seas Fleet (53 ships) scuttled in Scapa Flow (a body of water in the Orkney Islands, northern Scotland, United Kingdom, sheltered by the islands of Mainland, Graemsay, Burray, South Ronaldsay and Hoy), with nine deaths, the last casualties of the war.
June 28: Treaty of Versailles signed.
July 8: Germany ratifies the Treaty of Versailles.
July 21: The United Kingdom ratifies the Treaty of Versailles.
November 10-11: A Banquet in Honor of The President of the French Republic (Raymond Poincaré (1860-1934) President 1913-1920) was hosted by King George V (1865-1936, reign 1910-1936) and held at Buckingham Palace during the evening hours of November 10. The very first Armistice Day was held on the Grounds of Buckingham Palace on the Morning of November 11. This would set the trend for a day of Remembrance or Remembrance Day for decades to come.

24 April 1978, Oberwolfach (elevation 270 to 948 m, Black Forest), Germany, at Mathematisches Forschungsinstitut Oberwolfach.

Italy, 1 June 1978, Cortona: looking east to the northwest corner of the Basilica di Santa Margherita (right, 1288, 1330, 1738, 1878), and the south side of Fortezza Medicea (left up, 1556).

1920 Prohibition began on January 16 (one year after ratification of the amendment). Wilson felt Prohibition was unenforceable, but his veto of the Prohibition was overridden by Congress. By February 1920, the President's true condition was publicly known. At issue was Wilson's fitness for the presidency at a time when the League fight was reaching a climax, and domestic issues such as strikes, unemployment, inflation and the threat of Communism were ablaze. Because of this complex case, in 1967 the nation ratified the 25th Amendment, to allow the forcible replacement of an unable or unwilling incumbent President. In May, Wilson sent a long-deferred proposal to Congress to have the U.S. accept a mandate from the League of Nations to take over Armenia. He emphasized that the abandonment of Armenia was not his fault. An economic depression started and lasted 18 months.

January 10: First meeting of the League of Nations held in London. Official end of World War I.
Free City of Danzig established (1920-1939).
January 21: The Paris Peace Conference ends.
February 10: A plebiscite returns Northern Schleswig to Denmark.
April 19-26: Conference of Sanremo, north-western Italy, about League of Nations mandates in former Ottoman territories of the Middle East.
June 4: Treaty of Trianon (Grand Trianon Palace in Versailles) between the Allies and Hungary (the modern boundaries of Hungary are the same as those defined by the Treaty of Trianon, except for three villages that were transferred to Czechoslovakia in 1947).
August 10: Treaty of Sèvres (western Paris) between the Allies and the Ottoman Empire. The treaty is not recognized by the Turkish national movement, which considers the Istanbul government illegitimate.
November 1: League of Nations headquarters moved to Geneva, Switzerland.

2 May 2017, Fribourg (40,000 inhabitants), Switzerland, Mathematishes Institut or Département de mathématiques (the Faculty of Mathematics and Science was founded in 1896), Université de Fribourg (founded in 1889 by Georges Python (1856-1927), the only bilingual (French and German) university in Switzerland, five faculties, 10,000 students, 800 faculty), Chemin du Musée 23, close to the river La Sarine.

November 12: Treaty of Rapallo (a municipality in the province of Genoa, in Liguria, northern Italy, situated on the Ligurian Sea coast, on the Tigullio Gulf, between Portofino and Chiavari) between Italy and Yugoslavia. Zadar is annexed by Italy and the Free State of Fiume is established.

November 15: The League of Nations holds its first general assembly.

1921 After the end of his second term in 1921, Wilson and his wife moved from the White House to a nice 1915 town house in the Embassy Row section of Washington, D.C. Wilson was one of only two U.S. Presidents (Theodore Roosevelt was the first) to have served as president of the American Historical Association. He published short works on the international impact of the American Revolution, and the rise of totalitarianism.

The 29th U. S. President was Warren G. Harding: 1921-1923, 1865-1923 (57), U.S. Senator from Ohio.

Germán Arciniegas, 21, while a student, founded and managed the magazine *Universidad*.

Gheorghe Vrănceanu, 21, while a student, is named tutor.

October 13: Treaty of Kars (a city on a high plateau in northeastern Turkey, near the Armenian border) between Bolshevik Russia and Turkey.

1922 Wilson campaigned for Democratic candidates in the 1922 elections,

Gheorghe Vrănceanu, 22, graduates in Mathematics.

February 6: Washington Naval Treaty, limiting naval tonnage, signed by France, Italy, Japan, the United Kingdom and the United States.

24 April 1978, Oberwolfach (elevation 270 to 948 m, Black Forest), Germany, at Mathematisches Forschungsinstitut Oberwolfach.

Italy, 20 April 1978, Milano, in Piazza della Scala (Largo Antonio Ghiringhelli (1906-1979, left), looking northwest to the southeast façade of Teatro alla Scala (3 August 1778, capacity 2,800).

April 16: Treaty of Rapallo between Germany and Bolshevik Russia, to normalize diplomatic relations.

1923 In August, Wilson attended the funeral of his successor, Warren G. Harding. On November 10, Wilson made a short Armistice Day radio speech from the library of his home, his last national address. The following day he spoke briefly from the front steps, to more than 20,000 well wishers gathered outside the house.

The 30th U. S. President was Calvin Coolidge: 1923-1929, 1872-1933 (60), previously 29th Vice President of the United States.

Gheorghe Vrănceanu went to the University of Göttingen, Germany, where he studied under Professor David Hilbert. Thereafter, he went to the University of Rome, where he studied under Professor Tullio Levi-Civita.

July 24: Treaty of Lausanne (Switzerland) between the Allies and Turkey, successor State to the Ottoman Empire. It supersedes the Treaty of Sèvres.

1924 January 27: Treaty of Rome between Italy and Yugoslavia. Fiume is annexed by Italy, and the neighboring town of Sušak is assigned to Yugoslavia.

On February 3, Wilson died at home of a stroke and other heart-related problems at age 67. He was interred in a sarcophagus in Washington National Cathedral, and is the only president interred in the nation's capital. Mrs. Wilson stayed in the home another 37 years, dying there at age 89 on December 28, 1961, which was 105th Woodrow's birthday, and the day she was to be the guest of honor at the opening of the Woodrow Wilson Bridge across the Potomac River near Washington.

Arciniegas graduated from the National University of Colombia.

6 April 1978, Pisa, Palazzo della Carovana (1562-1564) now for Scuola Normale Superiore (1810, by Napoleon Bonaparte (1769-1821), 460 students, 6% admission rate, best in Italy).

6 April 1978, Pisa, Cattedrale di Pisa (1092, striped-marble, left), Torre di Pisa (August 1173-1372, 55.86 m on the low side, 56.67 m on the high side, white-marble, 296 steps, right).

Chapter 5. Professor Vranceanu

On November 5, Gheorghe Vrănceanu, 24, obtained his doctorate in Mathematics. He returned to Iaşi, where he was appointed a lecturer at the University of Iasi.

1927 Gheorghe Vrănceanu was awarded a Rockefeller scholarship to study in France (Sorbonne (1150 as a corporation associated with the cathedral school of Notre Dame de Paris, it was considered the second-oldest university in Europe.[1] Officially chartered in 1200 by King Philip II (Philippe-Auguste) of France and recognised in 1215 by Pope Innocent III, it was often nicknamed after its theology collegiate institution, College of Sorbonne, founded about 1257 by Robert de Sorbon and charted by Saint Louis, King of France; motto: Hic et ubique terrarum (Here and anywhere on Earth)), with Professor Elie Cartan). and the United States (Princeton and Harvard Universities, with Professor Weil)

August 1: Under the orders of the Russian dictator Stalin, the founding of the Chinese People's Liberation Army (PLA) took place, to serve the Communist Party of China (CPC), which was also created by Stalin.

1928 Germán Arciniegas, 28, joined El Tiempo, a daily newspaper in Bogotá, where he managed the editorial section, put together the Sunday Literary Supplement, and wrote a weekly column, becoming the general manager in 1937. He would continue to contribute articles and opinion pieces to El Tiempo for the rest of his life, speaking out against drug trafficking, Marxist guerrillas, and restrictive immigration policies.

1929 Arciniegas, 29, was vice consul in London, UK.

Gheorghe Vrănceanu received an offer to remain at Princeton, but he decided to return to Romania, and was appointed professor at the University of Cernăuți (at that time was in Romania; in 1940 was occupied by the Soviet Union, and now remained in Ukraine).

29 March 1978, Italy, Roma, COLVMNA·TRAIANI (113), commemorates Roman emperor Trajan's (53-117) victory in the Dacian Wars, constructed by Apollodorus of Damascus, located in Trajan's Forum, built near the Quirinal Hill, north of the Roman Forum; most famous for its spiral bas relief, which artistically describes the epic wars between the Romans and Dacians (101–102 and 105–106), 30 m in height, 35 m with pedestal, 20 colossal Carrara marble drums, each weighing about 32 tons, with a diameter of 3.7 m, 190-m frieze winds around the shaft 23 times, inside the shaft a spiral staircase of 185 steps provides access to a viewing platform at the top, the capital block of the column weighs 53.3 tons.

The 31st U. S. President was Herbert Hoover: 1929-1933, 1874-1964 (90), 3rd U.S. Secretary of Commerce

On June 18th, 1929, the British philosopher from the University of Oxford, John Randolph Lucas, was born in London.

On Thursday, October 24, began the Wall Street Crash of 1929, which is considered the beginning of the 10-year Great Depression that affected all Western industrialized countries.

1931. On February 1st Boris Yeltsin is born (President of Russia, died 2007), on March 2nd Mikhail Gorbachev is born (President of the Soviet Union, recipient of the Nobel Peace Prize), on May 1st the construction of the Empire State Building is completed in New York City. On June 3 Raul Castro is born (President of Cuba). On October 18 the American inventor Thomas Edison (born 1847) passed away at 84.

1932 Germán Arciniegas, 32, published his first book *El Estudiante de la Mesa Redonda* (The Student of the Round Table).

The President of the British Academy (1902) was John William Mackail (1859 – 1945, President 1932 – 1936, a scholar of Virgil (Publius Vergilius Maro, 70 BC in Cisalpine Gaul, Roman Republic – 19 BC in Brundisium, Roman Empire, very famous poet).

The positron (positive electron, the first known antiparticle of the electron) was discovered and photographed by the Nobel Laureate American Physicist Carl David Anderson (1905 – 1991).

On November 1st, Wernher von Braun (1912 – 1977), only 20 years old, was named the head of the German liquid-fuel rocket program.

Plato's quote: *Access to power must be confined to those who are not in love with it.*

20 Oct 1977, Venezia, Piazza San Marco, Il Campanile (center right) della Basilica Cattedrale Patriarcale di San Marco (with three of the five domes visible in center left, 1156 – 1173, last restored in 1514), rebuilt in 1912 *com'era, dov'era* (as it was, where it was) after the collapse of the original campanile on 14 July 1902 Palazzo Ducale (right),.

1933 The 32nd U. S. President was Franklin D. Roosevelt: 1933-1945, 1882-1945 (63), 44th Governor of New York.

The German president Paul von Hindenburg appoints Hitler (1889-1945) as chancellor, and 2 days later he dissolves the Parliament. On February 8th in the U. S., the first flight of all-metal Boeing 247 takes place, and the Congress repeals the alcohol Prohibition law. On March 6th Poland occupies the free city Danzig (Gdansk). German Reichstag grants Hitler dictatorial powers, and soon after Japan leaves the League of Nations. On May 10th Paraguay declares war on Bolivia. On August 30th Air France forms. In Cuba, Batista (1901-1973) becomes dictator at 32. On November 16, Brazilian President Getulio Vargas (1883-1954) declares himself dictator, and the United States recognizes the Soviet Union under Stalin (1878-1953), establishes diplomatic relations, and opens trade. To celebrate their recognition by the US, on November 25th the first Soviet liquid fuel rocket is launched, and reaches the altitude of 80 m   Fox Films in the US signs Shirley Temple (1928-2014), 5 years and 8 months old, to a studio contract (less than 4 months later Shirley Temple appears in her first movie, "Stand Up & Cheer").

1934. On February 9th, 1934, in Athens, Greece, the Pact of Balkan Entente alliance forms between Yugoslavia, Greece, Turkey and Romania, to defend themselves against territorial expansion, but the Soviet Union, Hungary, Bulgaria, Albania and Italy refused to sign the document.

A day later Stalin (1878-1953) ends the 17th congress of the Communist Party of the Soviet Union.

On March 1st, Henry Pu Yi is crowned emperor Kang Teh of Manchuria, by Japan.

Rudolf Kuhnold presents the first radar in Kiel, Germany, on March 20th.

Karlis Ulmanis names himself fascist dictator of Latvia on May 15th, 1934.

June 9th, the first Donald Duck cartoon, in Wise Little Hen, is released in the US.

2 May 1978, Fribourg, Switzerland, Fribourg Cathedral (right).

3 May 1978, Fribourg, Switzerland, near Université de Fribourg (founded in 1889 by Georges Python (1856-1927)).

RCA Victor releases the first 33 1/3 rotations/minute recording, with Ludwig van Beethoven's (1770-1827) Symphony Number 5 in Mi minor (1808).

Also the USSR joins the League of Nations, with the Netherlands, Switzerland and Portugal voting no.

On October 1st, 1934, Hitler expands German army and navy, and creates an air force, violating the 15 years old Treaty of Versailles (June 28, 1919).

On October 16th, Mao Zedong (1893-1976) and 25,000 troops begin the Long March (9000 km over 370 days) to retreat from the attacks of the troops of Chiang Kai-shek (1887-1975).

On December 29th Japan renounces the Washington Naval Treaty of 1922 (which limited naval construction) and the London Naval Treaty of 1930 (which regulated submarine warfare and limited naval shipbuilding).

Newton's quote: *Natura valde simplex est et sibi consona* - Nature is exceedingly simple and harmonious with itself.

1935 On December 21, Vrănceanu, 35, was elected full member of the Academy of Sciences of Romania.

The first US surgical operation for relief of angina pectoris was performed in Cleveland, and the inventor Edwin Armstrong gave the first public demonstration of FM broadcasting in the United States, at Alpine, New Jersey.

Prime Minister of the United Kingdom is Stanley Baldwin (1867 – 1947, PM 1935 – 1937, FRS, the only PM to have served under three monarchs (George V, Edward VIII and George VI)).

Plato's quote: *Necessity is the mother of invention.*

Nov 1993 Kyoto: Toji Temple, with a 5-story wooden pagoda, and sculptures of deities from around 750, 1 km southwest of Kyoto Tower.

Japan, Nov 1993, Osaka: very nice flower arrangement coming from a basket, near the north side of the Osaka Castle (1597, left up).

1936 Edward VIII (1894 – 1972) succeeds, on January 20, 1936, British king George V (1865 – 1936), but King Edward VIII marries Mrs. Wallis Simpson, and abdicates throne after 10 months and 22 days, on December 11, 1936. The Duke of York becomes, on December 11, 1936, King George VI (1895 – 1952).

The 11th Olympic Games take place in Berlin, August 1 – 16, 1936.

Germany and Japan sign the anti-Komintern pact.

After many Japanese attacks, the Chinese leader Chiang Kai-shek declares war on Japan.

Plato's quote: *Any man may easily do harm, but not every man can do good to another.*

1938 German troops invade Austria (Anschluss).
Instant coffee is invented in the US.

The Treaty of Munich is signed by Hitler, Mussolini (1883-1945), Daladier (1884 – 1970) and Chamberlain (1869 – 1940); Germany annexes Sudetenland (1/3 of Czechoslovakia).

Japanese troops occupy Canton, Hankou and Wuhan in China.

DuPont, in the US, announces its new synthetic fiber will be called "nylon".

Newton's quote: *Tact is the art of making a point without making an enemy.*

Italy, 5 Oct 1977, Torino (27 BC, 130 km², population 887,000, elevation 239 m, in Piedmont), looking east to Piazza Giambattista Bodoni (1740-1813, typographer), with his equestrian monument.

Italy, 18 Nov 1977, Roma, on the Pons Aelius (134 AD, 135 m, 7 m height, 5 spans, with 10 sculptures), over the river Tiber (Tevere), the Mausoleum of Hadrian (back, 134-139, Hadrian (76-138), after 650 wrongly called Castel Sant'Angelo).

1939   Gheorghe Vrănceanu, 39, moved to the University of Bucharest.

Solzhenitsyn, 21, is a student of mathematics at Rostov University in Russia. Rostov is one of the oldest towns in Russia, located on the north shores of Lake Nero, 200 km northeast of Moscow.

The uranium atom first split takes place at Columbia University, USA; Eugenio Pacelli was chosen as Pope Pius XII (1876 – 1958).

Germany occupies Czechoslovakia; Hungary annexes the republic of Karpato-Ukraine; the Sino-Japanese War (1937-1945) continues with the Battle of Nanchang; the Spanish Civil War ends and Madrid falls to Francisco Franco (1892 – 1975).

Faisal II (1935 – 1958) ascends to the throne of Iraq at the age of 4, and is the last King of Iraq; Italy invades Albania; Hungary leaves the League of Nations.

Stalin requests and then signs British-French-Soviet Union anti-nazi pact.

Germany and Italy announce an alliance known as the Rome-Berlin Axis.

The test flight of the first rocket plane, using liquid propellants, takes place in Germany.

The Russian offensive, under General Zhukov, against Japanese invasion in Mongolia, takes place.

Molotov-Ribbentrop pact: East Europe will be divided between Hitler and Stalin - Poland will be divided in half, Bessarabia from Romania will be occupied by Stalin; formally Germany and USSR sign a 10-year non-aggression pact.

Isoroku Yamamoto is appointed the supreme commander of the Japanese fleet; the Japanese invasion army is driven out of Mongolia by the Russians.

Italy, 16 Oct 1977, Bardonecchia (elevation 1,312 m, population 3200, 132 km², 90 km west of Torino, 100 km south of Mont Blanc (4808 m), Piedmont, western part of Susa Valley, it is the westernmost commune in Italy, at the Italian end of both the Fréjus Road Tunnel (1974-1980, 12.87 km) and the Fréjus Rail Tunnel (called Mont Cenis Tunnel, 13.7 km, 1974-1980, altitude 1123 m, under Pointe du Fréjus (2932 m), part of a TGV Paris to Milan.

The World War II (WW II) starts, Germany invades Poland, and takes Danzig • Britain declares war on Germany • France follows 6 hours later, quickly joined by Australia, New Zeeland, South Africa and Canada • Netherlands and Belgium declare neutrality • the USA declare themselves neutral • Iraq and Saudi Arabia declare war on Germany • Poland's president Moscicki and Prime Minister Slawoj-Skladkowski flee to Romania • Soviet Union invades Eastern Poland and takes 217,000 prisoners • Estonia accepts Soviet military bases • the Soviet-German treaty agrees on the 4th partition of Poland and gives Lithuania to the USSR • last Polish troops surrender, and Germany annexes Western Poland • Albert Einstein (1879 – 1955) informs the US President Roosevelt of the possibilities of an atomic bomb • four soviet soldiers are killed on the Finnish-Russian border, then the Soviet government revokes the Russian-Finnish non-attack treaty, and USSR invades Finland and bombs Helsinki • the League of Nations excludes the Soviet Union. Here=========

Churchill's quote: *It`s not enough that we do our best; sometimes we have to do what`s required.*

1940   Arciniegas, 40, was chancellor at the Colombian embassy in Argentina.
Solzhenitsyn, 22, marries Natalia, she divorces him in 1950, they marry again in 1957, and finally divorce in 1972.

Sergei Prokofiev's (1891 – 1953) ballet Romeo and Juliet premieres in Leningrad • Soviets bomb cities in Finland • the Polish pianist and composer Ignacy Jan Paderewski (1860 – 1941), Knight Grand Cross of the Order of the British Empire, at 80 becomes premier of the Polish government in exile • the first opera telecast, in New York City, is "I Pagliacci" (written in 1892) by Ruggero Leoncavallo (1857 – 1919) • Finland surrenders to the USSR and gives Karelische Isthmus • Mussolini joins Hitler in Germany's war against France and Britain • Karelo-Finnish SSR becomes the 12th Soviet republic (until 1956) • Germany invades Norway and Denmark (Denmark surrenders) • Italy annexes Albania • British troops land at Narvik, Norway •

Germany, 22 March 1978, Dortmund, in a nice square with water fountains, Der Neckermann (store, left), Apotheke (right).

Germany, 22 March 1978, Dortmund, the store Besta Hungshans (left), Avis rental service (center)

The first electron microscope is presented by RCA in Philadelphia, USA • Rear Admiral Joseph Taussig testifies, before the US Senate Naval Affairs Committee, that war with Japan is inevitable • Norwegian King Haakon VII (1872 – 1957, King for 52 years) and his government flee to England • the 1940 Olympics in Helsinki are cancelled • Winston Churchill (1874 – 1965) succeeds Neville Chamberlain as Prime Minister of United Kingdom (1940 – 1945) • German armies attack The Netherlands, Belgium and Luxembourg • Germany blitz conquest of France begins by crossing Meuse River (where World War 1 ended) • Dutch Queen Wilhelmina (1880 – 1962, Queen for nearly 58 years, starting at age 10) flees to England • Germany bombs Rotterdam, The Netherlands, (600 dead) • The Netherlands surrender to Germany • McDonald's opens its first restaurant in San Bernardino, California • Germany occupies Brussels, Belgium • French tanks counter attack at Pronne, under General Charles de Gaulle (1890 – 1970) • the first successful helicopter flight takes place in the US, with Vought-Sikorsky US-300, designed by the Russian American aviation pioneer Igor Ivanovich Sikorsky (1889 – 1972, immigrated to the US in 1919) • Operation Dynamo begins, to evacuate defeated Allied troops from Dunkirk, France • Belgium surrenders to Germany and King Leopold III (1901 – 1983) gives himself up • British-French troops capture Narvik in Norway • Premier Winston Churchill flies to Paris to meet with the 84 years old Marshal Philippe Pétain (1856 – 1951) , who announced he is willing to make a separate peace with Germany • German forces enter Paris • British and French troops evacuate Narvik in Norway • the discovery of the first chemical transuranic element with atomic number 93, neptunium (Np, a radioactive actinide metal, named after planet Neptune, itself named after Roman god of the sea Neptune), is announced in the US • General Charles de Gaulle's first meeting with Winston Churchill • Norway surrenders to Germany • Italy declares war on allies and raids Malta • in response, British forces bomb Genoa and Torino in Italy • France surrenders to Germany and German troops occupy Paris • Soviet Army occupies Lithuania and installs a communist government, then occupies Estonia •

Belgium, 19 March 1978, Bruxelles (990, by Charles, Duke of Lower Lorraine (953-993), capital of Belgium, population 1.1 M), from Grand Place looking southwest to the northeast façade of the Brussels Town Hall (Hôtel de Ville, 1402-1420, height 96 m). The façade is decorated with numerous statues representing nobles, saints, and allegorical figures (reproductions; the older ones are in the city museum in the "King's House" across the Grand Place).

Chapter 6. Professor Arciniegas, Minister

General Charles de Gaulle on BBC tells French people to defy the German occupiers • France signs an armistice with Italy • USSR ends the use of an experimental calendar, and returns to Gregorian calendar • Soviet Army attacks Romania and Romania cedes Bessarabia to the Soviet Union • Hitler orders invasion of England (Operation Sealion) • British Royal Navy sinks the French fleet in North Africa • the diplomatic relations are broken between Britain and Vichy government in France • Battle of Britain begins as German forces attack by air for 114 days • Soviet Union annexes Estonia, Latvia and Lithuania • Italian troops invade British Somalia (in the Horn of Africa, near the Gulf of Aden) • Churchill recognizes De Gaulle French government in exile • Alsace Lorraine from France is annexed by the Third Reich (name for Germany from 1933 to 1945) • Greece mobilizes • General George Marshall is sworn in as chief of staff of the US army • the first showing of the high definition color TV takes place in the USA • Crown prince (19 years old) Mihai (Michael, born 1921) succeeds Carol II as king of Romania • 4 teens, going down a hole near Lascaux, France, discover 17,000-year-old drawings, now known as the Lascaux Cave Paintings • Japanese troops attack French Indo-China • Germany, Italy and Japan sign a 10 year formal alliance (Axis) • German troops occupy Romania • 40 hour work week goes into effect in the USA • Italy attacks Greece, but Greece successfully resists • Hungary, Romania and Slovakia join the Axis Powers • • British troops have their first major offensive in North Africa • Germany begins dropping incendiary bombs on London.

Churchill's quote: *Never in the field of human conflict was so much owed by so many to so few.*

1941 Germán Arciniegas, 41, was briefly Minister of Education, until mid 1942.

Canada and US acquire air bases in Newfoundland (99 years lease) • Kuomintang forces under orders from Chiang Kai-Shek open fire at communist forces, resuming the Chinese Civil War • British offensive in Eritrea takes place •

23 March 1978, Freibourg im Breisgau (1120 by Duke Berthold III of Zähringen (1085-1122), elevation 278 m, the south façade of Freiburger Münster (cathedral, 1200, 116 m, J S Bach (1685-1750)).

Germany, 20 March 1978, Dortmund, Dortmunder Union Bier (left), Scheda (left), on a busy street only for pedestrians.

British and Australian troops capture Tobruk, North Africa, from Italians • British troops march into Abyssinia (Ethiopian Empire) • Japanese armored barges cross Strait of Johore to attack Singapore • Plutonium is first produced and isolated by the American chemist, with Nobel Prize in Chemistry, Dr. Glenn T. Seaborg (1912 – 1999) • German troops invade Bulgaria, then Bulgaria joined the Axis Pact • 50,000 British soldiers land in Greece • Britain leases defense bases in Trinidad (near Venezuela) to US for 99 years • Churchill warns Stalin of a plan for a German invasion of the USSR • the operation Bestrafung begins - Germany bombers attack Belgrade, Yugoslavia, 17,000 die • Italian held Addis Abeba (Ethiopia) surrenders to British and Ethiopian forces • pact of neutrality between the USSR and Japan is signed • the Kingdom of Yugoslavia surrenders to Germany • Bulgarian troops invade Macedonia in Greece • 100 German bombers attack Athens, Greece • Greece surrenders to Germany • Operation Merkur: Hitler orders the conquest of Crete (the largest Greek island, in the south) • Stalin becomes premier of USSR • Konrad Zuse presents the Z3, the world's first working programmable, fully automatic computer, in Berlin • the first British turbojet flies • Italian army under General Aosta surrenders to Britain at Amba Alagi, Ethiopia • Germany invades Crete, Greece • British troops attack Baghdad, Iraq • the USA declares state of emergency, due to Germany's sinking of the US ship Robin Moor • a German Luftwaffe air raid on Dublin, Ireland, claims 38 lives • Germany bans all Catholic publications • English and French troops overthrow the pro-German Syrian government • Estonians start armed resistance against the Soviet occupation • Finland invades Karelia • Operation Barbarossa: Germany attacks the Soviet Union and occupies the Baltic states • Germany, Italy, Romania and Finland declare war on the Soviet Union • US forces land in Iceland to forestall Germany invasion • Beirut, Lebanon, is occupied by Free France and British troops • the pharmaceutical-grade penicillin is produced in large quantities by Pfizer in Brooklyn, New York, USA • British Prime Minister Winston Churchill launched his "V for Victory" campaign • the USA demand Japanese troops out of Indo-China and start embargo on oil-export to Japan •

23 March 1978, Freibourg im Breisgau (1120 by Duke Berthold III of Zähringen (1085-1122), elevation 278 m), from Münsterplatz looking west to the eastern main entrance and façade of Freiburger Münster (cathedral, 1200, 116 m, Johann Sebastian Bach (1685-1750) played the later versions of Passio Domini nostri J.C. secundum Evangelistam Matthæum (Matthäuspassion (St Matthew Passion)) in 1743 in this cathedral).

The US President Franklin Roosevelt and British Prime Minister Winston Churchill issue the joint declaration that later becomes known as the Atlantic Charter • German troops reach Leningrad • English and Russian troops attack pro-German Iran and Reza Shah Pahlavi (1878 – 1944) of Iran is forced to abdicate throne to his son Mohammad Reza Pahlavi (1919 – 1980) • the blockade of Leningrad (St. Petersburg) by Germany begins • Roosevelt orders any Axis ships found in American waters to be shot on sight • the U.S. Navy is ordered to attack German U-boats • the construction of the Pentagon for the US Department of Defense begins (completed on January 15, 1943) • General de Gaulle forms the French government in exile in London • nine Allied governments pledge adherence to the common principles of the policy set forth in the Atlantic Charter • German troops start an assault on Moscow: operation Taifun begins • USA lends Soviet Union $1 million • Germany's drive to take Moscow is halted • Mussolini's forces leave Abyssinia (Ethiopia) • Japanese emperor Hirohito (1901 – 1989) secretly signs declaration of war against the USA on December 1st, 1941 • German siege of Tobruk (port in Libya, near Egypt), after 8 months, ends • Japanese attack Pearl Harbor, Hawaii, USA, on December 7, 1941 • in London, the Dutch government in exile declares war on Japan and Italy • the US and Britain declare war on Japan, and the USA enters the World War II • China declares war on Germany and Italy • Germany and Italy declare war on the USA • Dutch and Australian troops land on the island Portuguese Timor (south of Indonesia, 500 km north of Australia) • German troops led by the field marshal Erwin Rommel (1891 – 1944) begin retreating in North Africa • Japanese troops land on Hong Kong • Hitler takes complete command of the German Army • Premier Winston Churchill arrives in Washington, DC, for a wartime conference • Japan announces the surrender of the British-Canadian garrison in Hong Kong • Winston Churchill becomes the first British Prime Minister to address a joint meeting of the Congress of the USA, warning that the Axis would "stop at nothing" • Japan bombs Manila, capital of Philippines, even though it was declared an "open city" • Winston Churchill addresses the Canadian parliament.

Italy, 18 Dec 1977, Bardonecchia (1312 m, population 3200, 90 km west of Torino, 100 km south of Mont Blanc (4808 m)).

Italy, 18 Dec 1977, Bardonecchia (1312 m, population 3200, 90 km west of Torino, 100 km south of Mont Blanc (4808 m)).

Churchill's quote: *Never, never, never give up.*

1942   Solzhenitsyn, 24, is an artillery captain in the Russian army for 2.5 years during World War II.

The USA, UK and 24 other countries sign a united declaration against the Axis   •   28 nations, at war with the Axis, pledge no separate peace   •   German troops in Bardia, a seaport in Libya near Egypt, surrender   •   Japanese troops occupy Manila, Philippines   •   the first US forces in Europe during WW II go ashore in Northern Ireland   •   Hitler's Operation Sealion (invasion of England) is cancelled   •   about 150 Japanese warplanes attack the north Australian city of Darwin   •   the US President Roosevelt orders detention and internment of all west-coast Japanese-Americans   •   the US President Franklin Roosevelt orders General Douglas MacArthur (1880 – 1964) out of the Philippines, as American defenses collapse   •   one Japanese submarine fires on an oil refinery in Ellwood, 50 km west of Los Angeles, California, USA   •   the English physicist and radio astronomer James Stanley Hey (1909 – 2000), Fellow of the Royal Society, discovers radio emissions from the Sun   •   Roosevelt orders men between 45 and 64 to register for non-military duty   •   the British Arctic convoy PQ13, with war supplies on 19 British, American and Polish ships, departs Reykjavik, Iceland, to Murmansk, USSR, where only 15 ships arrived (during the war about 1400 ships delivered essential war supplies to the USSR)   •   The US move native-born of Japanese ancestry into detention centers   •   Tokyo is bombed by American airplanes   •   the Battle of the Coral Sea (off the northeast coast of Australia) ends, stopping Japanese expansion   •   a helicopter makes its first cross-country flight in the USA   •   Mexico declares war on Germany and Japan   •   Anglo-Soviet Treaty is signed in London   •

Germany, 23 March 1978, looking west to Neuenburg am Rhein, near the border with France, Mullheim ahead (west), Breisach left (north), Schliengen right (south).

Germany, 20 March 1978, Dortmund, Pezzer (center), Pelze (left).

Battle of Midway (territory of the US, an atoll in the North Pacific Ocean, equidistant between North America and Asia, about one-third of the way from Honolulu, Hawaii to Tokyo, Japan) begins, and this is Japan's first major defeat in WW II, just six months after Japan's attack on Pearl Harbor, Hawaii • USA declares war on Bulgaria, Hungary and Romania • Japanese troops land on the islands Kiska and Attu (2500 km northeast of Japan and 2000 km southwest of continental Alaska), Aleutian Islands, Alaska, USA • German troops march into Sevastopol, a port on the Black Sea, in the southwestern region of the Crimean Peninsula, USSR • the German army is defeated by the British army at El-Alamein, port in Egypt, on the Mediterranean Sea, 106 km west of Alexandria • the US and USSR sign the Lend-Lease agreement during WW II, which gives to the USSR much needed war military assistance from the US • the first V-2 rocket is launched at Peenemunde Army Research Center (Heeresversuchsanstalt Peenemunde), on the Baltic Sea island of Usedorn, 250 km north of Berlin, Germany, and reached 1.3 km • Germany occupies Egypt • Major General Dwight Eisenhower (1890 – 1969) is appointed commander of the US forces in Europe • the US air offensive against Germany begins • Netherland's government in exile (London) recognizes the Soviet Union • the first American offensive in Pacific starts at Guadalcanal, the principal island of the Solomon Islands, in the south-western Pacific, 1500 km northeast of Australia • Field Marshal Bernard Montgomery (1887 – 1976) becomes commandant of the British army in North Africa • British premier Churchill arrives in Moscow and meets Stalin • Dwight D Eisenhower is named commander for invasion of North Africa • Premier Churchill travels back to Cairo from Moscow • the US 8th Air Force bombs occupied Europe for the first time • Generalfeldmarschall Fredrich Paulus (1890 – 1957, married Elena Rosetti-Solescu in 1912 (she died in 1949, in Baden)) orders German 6th Army to conquer Stalingrad • Brazil declares war on Germany, Japan and Italy •

Italy, 23 Oct 1977, Bardonecchia (elevation 1,312 m, 90 km west of Torino, Piedmont, western part of Susa Valley) Traforo Fréjus Cogefar-Cogeco, railway Frejus tunnel, the first crossing the Alps.

Italy, 23 Oct 1977, Bardonecchia (1312 m, population 3200, 90 km west of Torino), looking west to the Alps, after which is France.

The Battle of Stalingrad starts: 600 German Luftwaffe bomb Stalingrad and 40,000 die • Cuba declares war on Germany, Japan and Italy • Germany annexes Luxembourg • German troops enter Stalingrad • Japanese planes drop incendiary bombs on Oregon, north of California, USA • British troops land on the island of Madagascar, 500 km east of Mozambique in southeast Africa • Russian troops organize a counter offensive at Stalingrad • launch of the first A-4/V-2 rocket to the altitude of 85 km takes place in Germany • the first salvo of the Russian Katjoesja-rocket destroys a German battalion in Stalingrad • the US and British governments announce the establishment of the United Nations • the first WW II American expeditionary force lands in Africa • last Vichy-French troops in Algeria surrender (Vichy is 400 km south of Paris) • 1 million Russians breach the German lines • 3rd and 5th Romanian army corps surrender • German 4th and 6th Army are surrounded at Stalingrad • Japan bombs again the Port Darwin, in the north of Australia • Josip Broz Tito (1892 – 1980) appoints Anti-fascist Liberation Committee in Yugoslavia • the first controlled nuclear chain reaction is done by the Italian physicist Enrico Fermi (1901 – 1954) at the University of Chicago.

Churchill's quote: *Courage is rightly esteemed the first of human qualities... because it is the quality which guarantees all others.*

1943 The US and Britain relinquish extraterritorial rights in China • Roosevelt and Churchill confer in Casablanca (the largest city in the western Morocco, on the Atlantic Ocean, 300 km southwest of Gibraltar) concerning WW II • the world's largest office building, with air conditioning system, the Pentagon (for the US Department of Defense), was completed • pre-sliced bread sale is banned in the US, to reduce bakery demand for metal parts • Soviets announce that they broke the long German siege of Leningrad (now Saint Petersburg, in the east of the Gulf of Finland in the Baltic Sea, 300 km east of Helsinki), where over one million city residents died • the US ration bread and metal •

Italy, 18 Nov 1977, Roma, COLVMNA·TRAIANI (113), commemorates Roman emperor Trajan's (53-117) victory in the Dacian Wars, constructed by Apollodorus of Damascus, located in Trajan's Forum, built near the Quirinal Hill, north of the Roman Forum; most famous for its spiral bas relief, which artistically describes the epic wars between the Romans and Dacians (101–102 and 105–106), 30 m in height, 35 m with pedestal, 20 colossal Carrara marble drums, each weighing about 32 tons, with a diameter of 3.7 m, 190-m frieze winds around the shaft 23 times, inside the shaft a spiral staircase of 185 steps provides access to a viewing platform at the top, the capital block of the column weighs 53.3 tons.

The Battle of Anzio (a small city on the Tyrhenian Sea, in the southwest Italy, 56 km south of Rome) takes place, and Allies are stopped on the beach, by the Germans, until 1944 • British 8th army marches into Tripoli, Libya • Field Marshal Friedrich von Paulus surrenders to the Russian troops at Stalingrad, and the battle of Stalingrad ends with the final surrender of the German 6th Army • shoe rationing begins in the US • Japanese evacuate Guadalcanal • The U.S. President Franklin Roosevelt, in an attempt to check inflation, freezes wages and prices, prohibits workers from changing jobs, unless the war effort would be aided thereby, and bars rate increases to common carriers and public utilities • Soviet Union breaks contact with the Polish government exiled in London • 5th German Pantzer army surrenders in Tunisia • US 7th division lands on Attu, Aleutian Islands, the first US territory recaptured from Japanese troops • Axis forces in North Africa surrender • Stalin dissolves the Comintern (Communist International, founded by Lenin in 1919) • The United States Army contracts with the University of Pennsylvania's Moore School to develop the ENIAC computer • British troops invade Pantelleria, Italy, (a tiny island, the ancient Cossyra, 100 km southwest of Sicily, and 60 km east of the Tunisian coast) • Allies begin 10-day bombing on Hamburg, north Germany • the US forces land at Nassau Bay, near the small town Salamaua, Papua New Guinea, 800 km northeast of Australia • the Battle of Kursk (USSR, 400 km northeast of Kiev and 600 km southwest of Moscow) begins, involving 6,000 tanks • the US invasion fleet (96 ships) sails to Sicily, Italy, and US, British and Canadian forces invade Sicily (Operation Husky) • after 8 days of heavy fighting, the greatest tank battle in history ends with the USSR victory over Germany at Kursk, where almost 6,000 tanks took part, and 2,900 were lost by Germany • the Royal Air Force (RAF) bombs Germany rocket base at Peenemunde • 500 allied air forces raid Rome, Italy •

Italy, 11 Feb 1978, looking north to Spiaggia (Beach) di Mondello and Tyrrhenian Sea, 10 km northwest of Palermo, Sicilia.

Italy, 13 Feb 1978, on a boat in Messina, Sicilia Island, moving east to Villa San Giovanni (left back), north of Reggio Calabria.

The US forces led by General George Patton liberate Palermo, northwest of Sicily, Italy • Benito Mussolini is captured and dismissed as premier of Italy • during the Battle of Troina, (center-east of Sicily, 60 km northwest of Catania), Mount Etna (3350 m, 40 km east of Troina) erupts, sending ash and lava many kilometers into the sky • Japan leaves Aleutian Islands, west Alaska, USA • German occupiers impose 72-hour work (over 10 hours/day, all days) week in occupied countries • Lord Mountbatten (1900 – 1979) is appointed Supreme Allied Commander in South East Asia • British 8th army lands in south Italy at Messina (Sicily) • Italy surrenders to the Allies in WW II • US, British and French troops land in Salerno (city on the Gulf of Salerno on the Tyrrhenian Sea, 50 km southeast of Naples (Napoli), Italy) (operation Avalanche) • German troops occupy Rome and take over the protection of the Vatican City • having been Generalissimo since 1928, Chiang Kai-shek becomes president of China • Great Britain establishes bases on the Archipelago of the Azores, in the North Atlantic Ocean, 1360 km west of Portugal • Italy declares war on its former Axis partner Germany • streptomycin, the first antibiotic remedy for tuberculosis, is isolated by researchers at Rutgers University, New Brunswick, New Jersey, USA • the first US ambassador to Canada, Ray Atherton (1883 – 1960), is nominated • 444 British bombers attack Berlin, Germany • US forces land on Tarawa and Makin Atoll in the Gilbert Islands (in the central Pacific Ocean, 3500 km northeast of Australia, and 4000 km southwest of Hawaii) • Roosevelt, Churchill and Chiang Kai-shek meet to discuss ways to defeat Japan • Lebanon declares independence from the French administration • Conference of Teheran (Iran, 1190 m, 100 km south of the Caspian Sea, 1600 km southeast of Stalingrad (now Volgograd)) between Churchill, Roosevelt and Stalin, takes place • the second conference of Cairo, Egypt: Roosevelt, Churchill and Turkish president Inonu (1884 – 1973), takes place • Roosevelt appoints General Eisenhower the supreme commander of the Allied forces in Europe.

Belgium, 19 March 1978, Bruxelles (990, population 1.1 M), from Grand Place looking to the northwest façade of a classical building.

27 March 1978, Bulle, 771 m, Switzerland, 40 km northeast of Lausanne, 30 km south of Fribourg, 3 km west of Lac de la Gruyère.

Churchill's quote: *All the great things are simple, and many can be expressed in a single word: freedom, justice, honor, duty, mercy, hope.*

1944   The first use of helicopters during warfare (British Atlantic patrol) takes place   •   the US Air Force announces the production of the first US jet fighter, the Bell P-59   •   The first mobile electric power plant is delivered in Philadelphia, USA   •   Churchill and de Gaulle begin a two-day wartime conference in Marrakesh (major city in southeast Morocco, 600 km southwest of Gibraltar)   •   British Royal Air Force drops 2300 tons of bombs on Berlin   •   447 German bombers attack London   •   649 British bombers attack Magdeburg (an old medieval city on the Elbe River, 160 km southwest of Berlin, Germany)   •   Leningrad is liberated from the German blockade, after 880 days, with over 1,000,000 civilians killed   •   683 British bombers attack Berlin   •   285 German bombers attack London   •   Italian town of Cassino, 2 km east of Monte Cassino, is destroyed by Allied bombing   •   Germany occupies Hungary   •   Mount Vesuvius (1281 m, 9 km east of Naples, Italy) erupts (the last eruption so far)   •   Japanese troops conquer Jessami, a small village in East-India, elevation 1200 m   •   the Soviet Army marches into Romania   •   British troops capture Addis Abeba, Ethiopia, from Italians   •   De Gaulle forms a new govern in exile   •   Allies bomb Bucharest, targeting railroads, and kill 5,000 people   •   Generals Rommel, Speidel and von Stulpnagel attempt to assassinate Hitler   •   the Polish 2nd Army corp captures the convent of Monte Cassini, Italy   •   the German defense line in Italy collapses   •   Icelandic voters sever all ties with Denmark   •   the Japanese advance in Hangzhou, China, northwest of the Qiantang River, 150 km southwest of Shanghai   •   the Germans pull out of Rome, Italy   •   the US 5th Army enters and liberates Rome from Mussolini's Fascist armies   •   King Victor Emmanuel III of Italy (1869 – 1947) abdicates the power, and then the throne remains for his son Umberto II (1904 – 1983, last king of Italy (only for 34 days))   •

1 Jan 1978, Pisa, from the west part of Piazza del Duomo, looking east to Torre di Pisa (August 1173-1372, 55.86 m on the low side, 56.67 m on the high side, white-marble, 296 steps, lavishly adorned Leaning Tower of Pisa, il campanile of the cathedral, prior to restoration (1990-2001) leaned at an angle of 5.5 degrees, now leans at 3.99 degrees, the top is displaced horizontally 3.9 m from the center, Galileo Galilei (1564-1642) used the tower for experiments, center), Cattedrale di Pisa (1092, left, striped-marble).

D-Day: 150,000 Allied Expeditionary Force lands in Normandy, France   •   the Russian offensive in Karelia (on the border with Finland) takes place   •   15 US aircraft carriers attack Japanese bases on Marianas Islands (2000 km southeast of Japan, west of the Mariana Trench, the deepest part of the oceans (-10971 m)   •   the first German V-1 rocket assault on London takes place   •   the first B-29 bomber raid against mainland Japan takes place   •   the US forces begin the invasion of Saipan (part of the Northern Mariana Islands in Pacific, 2500 km south east of Japan)   •   Iceland declares independence from Denmark   •   Japanese troops conquer Changsha (on Xiang River, a branch of the Yangtze River, 900 km southwest of Shanghai, China)   •   the US Congress charters the Central Intelligence Agency   •   more than 2500 people are killed in London and South-East England by German V-1 flying bombs   •   the United Nations Monetary and Financial Conference (1 – 22 July 1944, 730 delegates from 44 Allied nations) at Bretton Woods (12 km west of Mount Washington (1917 m), 250 km north of Boston, USA) starts, establishing the International Monetary Fund and the World Bank. The Bretton Woods system worked for 27 years, until 1971.

Mount Washington Resort, Bretton Woods, New Hampshire, USA, where the United Nations Monetary and Financial Conference took place in July 1944.

• the British troops march into Caen (northwest of France, 20 km south of the English Channel, 400 km west of Paris)   • the US government recognizes the authority of General De Gaulle   • Vilnius (200 km northwest of Minsk), the capital of Lithuania (south of Latvia, northeast of Poland, west of Russia (now Belarus), is liberated by the Russian troops, which also cross the river Bug, the border with Poland   • the first German V-2 rocket hits Great Britain   • the first British jet fighter is used in combat (Gloster Meteor)   • Turkey breaks diplomatic relationship with Germany   • British 8th army reaches the suburbs of Florence (central Italy, 300 km northwest of Rome)   • IBM dedicates, in the US, the first program-controlled calculator, the Automatic Sequence Controlled Calculator (known best as the Harvard Mark I)   • Churchill and Tito meet in Naples (200 km southeast of Rome, Italy)   • Operation Anvil: Allies land on the French Mediterranean sea coast, to liberate Montpellier, Marseille, and Nice   • Operation Dragoon: Allied troops land in Provence (southeast of France)   •

the Russian troops arrive at the Austrian border   •   the last Japanese troops are driven out of India   •   the Russian offensive arrives at Jassy and Kishinev, northeast of Romania   •   Allied troops capture Marseilles, France   •   King Mihai (Michael) of Romania (born 1921, king 1927 – 1930 and 1940 – 1947) orders his forces to cease fire against Allies and dismisses the pro-Axis premier, Marshal Ion Antonescu (1882 – 1946)   •   a tank division of the British Guards frees Brussels, capital of Belgium, 300 km northeast of Paris   •   Finland breaks diplomatic contact with Germany   •   Belgium, Luxembourg and Netherlands sign unity treaty   •   the first German V-2 rockets land in London and Antwerp (Belgium, 50 km north of Brussels)   •   Russians march into Bulgaria and Bulgaria declares war on Germany   •   Allied forces liberate Luxembourg   •   Roosevelt and Churchill meet in Canada at the second Quebec Conference   •   British troops land on Greek territory   •   Canadians free Austria   •   Soviets march into Hungary and Czechoslovakia   •   British Prime Minister Winston Churchill arrives in the USSR for talks with Stalin   •   US takes the Japanese island Okinawa (1500 km southwest of Tokyo)   •   Tannu Tuva (south of Russia, northwest of Mongolia) is annexed by the U.S.S.R.   •   German army retreats from Athens, Greece   •   Allied troops land in Corfu (western Greece, 100 km southeast of Italy)   •   British troops march into Athens, Greece   •   John Hopkins hospital in the USA performs the first open heart surgery   •   General De Gaulle arrives in Moscow   •   British order to disarm everybody in Greece, causes general strike there   •   the Greek Civil War breaks out in a newly-liberated Greece, between communists and royalists   •   Japanese-Americans are released from the detention camps in the US (in 1988 President Ronal Reagan (1911 – 2004) signed a law which apologized for the internment, and paid over $1.6 billions in reparations)   •   Battle of Bastogne (city in southwest Belgium, at the border with Luxembourg): Germans surround the US 101st Airborne   •   The US General Patton's 4th Tank division turns away the German army at Bastogne   •   Budapest, Hungary, is surrounded by the Soviet army   •   King George II of Greece (1890 – 1947, spouse Elisabeth of Romania) abdicates his throne   •   Hungary declares war on Germany.

Italy, 1 Oct 1977, Firenze, in Piazza del Duomo, looking east at the south part of the west colored marble façade of Cattedrale of Santa Maria del Fiore (9 Sep 1296 – 25 March 1436, left, called il Duomo di Firenze, length 153 m, width 90 m, height 114 m, floor area 8,300 m^2), red-tiled Filippo Brunelleschi's (1377-1446) Dome (center up), and distinctive Giotto's (1266-1337) Campanile (1334, right, square in plan with 14.45 m sides, 84.7 m tall, with seven bells).

Churchill's quote: *The price of greatness is responsibility.*

1945   Germán Arciniegas, 45, was briefly Minister of Education until mid 1946. He founded the Caro and Cuervo Institute and moved the Colombian National Museum to its current home in a former prison building.

The 33rd U. S. President was Harry S. Truman: 1945-1953, 1884-1972 (88), 34th Vice President of the U.S.

Solzhenitsyn, 27, is arrested for "disrespectful remarks" written about Stalin in correspondences with a friend. He is taken to a labor camp in Russia for an eight-year sentence.

British Premier Winston Churchill visits France • US soldiers led by General Douglas MacArthur (1880 – 1964) invade Philippines • German forces in Belgium retreat in the Battle of Bulge • The Soviets begin a large offensive against the Germans in Eastern Europe • the liberation of Warsaw by the Soviet troops takes place • Roosevelt, Churchill and Stalin meet at Yalta (a Russian resort city in the south of the Crimean peninsula, on the north coast of the Back Sea, 30 km east of Sevastopol, 500 km east of Constanta (Romania)) • US troops under General Douglas MacArthur enter Manila, Philippines • Russian Red Army crosses the river Oder, which forms part of the border between Poland and Germany, in the middle being 100 km east of Berlin • the US 76th and 5th Infantry divisions begin crossing river Sauer, which is in Belgium, Luxemburg and Germany, a left tributary of the river Moselle, and forms a part of the border between Luxemburg and Germany, 200 km west of Frankfurt • Allied planes bomb Dresden, in eastern Germany, 200 km south of Berlin, 135,000 die • The USSR captures Budapest (capital of Hungary, 300 km southeast of Vienna, Austria), after 49-day battle with German troops: 159,000 die • Peru, Paraguay, Chile and Ecuador join the United Nations • Venezuela declares war on Germany •

Italy, 25 Sep 1977, Bologna (1000 BC, 140 km^2, elevation 54 m, metro population 1 M, the capital and largest city of the Emilia-Romagna region in Northern Italy, with the oldest university in the world, University of Bologna, founded in 1088), northwest of Piazza Maggiore, in Piazza del Nettuno, looking north to the southern part of Fontana del Nettuno (1565, bronze sculpture by Giambologna (1529-1608, Flemish sculptor Jean Boulogne based in Italy)).

30,000 US Marines land on the Japanese island Iwo Jima (Sulfur Island, only 21 km², 1200 km south of Tokyo) • Queen Wilhelmina (1880 – 1962) returns to the Netherlands • Würzburg, central Germany (100 km southeast of Frankfurt), is 90% destroyed, with 5,000 dead, in only 20 minutes, by British bombers • 1,250 US bombers attack Berlin • Hitler issues the Nero Decree to destroy all German factories • the first Japanese flying bombs (ochas) attack US Navy ships near the Japanese island Okinawa (1500 km southwest of Tokyo) • the largest operation in the Pacific war: 1,500 US Navy ships bomb Okinawa, Japan • the Japanese resistance ends on Iwo Jima • the US 20th Army corp captures Wiesbaden, central Germany, on Rhein river, 20 km west of Frankfurt • the last German V-1 (buzz bomb) attack on London • the USSR invades Austria • the 32nd US President Franklyn D. Roosevelt dies (January 30, 1882 – April 12, 1945) • Harry Truman (1884 – 1972) is sworn in as the 33rd President of the USA • the Red Army occupies Wien (Vienna), Austria • American planes bomb Tokyo and damage the Imperial Palace • the US 7th Army and allies forces capture Nuremberg and Stuttgart in southern Germany • the Red Army begins the Battle of Berlin • Benito Mussolini flees from Salò (a small town on the central-west banks of Lago di Garda, 100 km east of Milano), to Milano • delegates from 46 countries gather in San Francisco for the United Nations Conference on International Organization • the last Boeing B-17 attack against Germany takes place • the Red Army completely surrounds Berlin • the US and Soviet forces meet at Torgau, Germany, on the Elbe River, 200 km southwest of Berlin • Marshal Henri Philippe Pétain (1856 – 1951), leader of France's Vichy collaborationist regime during WW II, is arrested for treason • Italian partisans capture and execute Benito Mussolini (July 29, 1883 – April 28, 1945) • the US 5th army enters Genoa, northwest Italy, port on the Ligurian Sea, 150 km south of Milano • the Völkischer Beobachter, the newspaper of the Nazi Party in Germany, ceases publication • the US 5th army reaches the Swiss border • the Japanese army evacuates Rangoon in Burma (now Yangon in Myanmar, 300 km west of Thailand) •

Italy, 26 Jan. 1978, Vale d'Aosta, list of hotels before Saint Didier (1004 m), Palleusieux (1108 m), Verrand (1267 m), Mont Blanc (Monte Bianco, 4,808 m, in France, Graian Alps, between the regions of Aosta Valley, Italy, and Savoie and Haute-Savoie, France. very close to Italy, the highest mountain in the Alps, and the highest in Europe west of Russia's Caucasus peaks, 11th in the world in topographic prominence) is left up, 15 km to the northwest.

The Terms of surrender of the German armies in Italy is signed • Admiral Karl Doenitz (1891 – 1980) forms a new German government • the Soviet army reaches Rostock, north Germany, on the Baltic Sea, 300 km northwest of Berlin • the German Army in Italy surrenders • the Soviet Union takes Berlin: General Weidling (1891 – 1955), the last commander of the Berlin Defense Area, surrenders, Adolf Hitler (April 20, 1889 – April 30, 1945) kills himself • Yugoslav troops occupy Trieste, seaport on the Adriatic Sea, in northeastern Italy, 150 km east of Venezia (Venice) • German Field Marshal General Von Keitel (1882 – 1946) formally surrenders to the Russian Marshal Zhukov (1896 – 1974) • Victory in Europe Day: Germany signs unconditional surrender, World War II ends in Europe • German archipelago of Helgoland (170 ha), in the southeastern corner of the North Sea, 200 km northwest of Hamburg, surrenders to the British troops • the US, USSR, UK and France agree to split occupied Germany, and they declare supreme authority over Germany • The US forces defeat the Japanese forces in the Japanese island Okinawa • The United Nations Charter is signed by 50 nations in San Francisco, USA • The Polish Provisional government of National Unity is set up by the Soviets • Ruthenia, formerly in the eastern Czechoslovakia, becomes part of the USSR • the Labour Party wins the British parliamentary election • the liberation of the Philippines is officially declared • the first test detonation of a plutonium bomb takes place at Trinity Site, Alamogordo (200 km south of Albuquerque), New Mexico, USA, on July 16, 1945 at 5:30 AM • Potsdam (25 km southwest of Berlin) Conference, with Truman, Stalin and Churchill, holds its first meeting • Declaration of Potsdam: USA, UK and China demand Japanese surrender, but the Japanese government disregards the ultimatum • Winston Churchill resigns as UK's Prime Minister. Clement Attlee (1883 – 1967, PM 1945 – 1951, FRS) • the US Senate ratifies the United Nations charter 89-2 • the atomic bomb is dropped on Hiroshima (western Japan, 800 km southwest of Tokyo) on Aug 6th, to force Japan to surrender • the US, USSR, England and France sign the Treaty of London regarding the International Military Tribunal •

29 March 1978, Italy, Roma (753 BC, one of the oldest occupied cities in Europe, called Roma Aeterna (The Eternal City) and Caput Mundi (Capital of the World)), inside Amphitheatrum Flavium (80, started by Flavius Vespasian (born 9 AD, emperor 69-79) in 70, and completed by his son Titus Flavius Vespasianus (born 39, emperor 79-81), built of concrete and sand, it is the largest amphitheater ever built, for 80,000 spectators, wrongly called Colosseum).

The USSR declares war against Japan and then establishes communist governments in China and in North Korea • the USA drop the second atomic bomb on Japan and destroy part of Nagasaki (western Japan, 1000 km southwest of Tokyo, 300 km southwest of Hiroshima) • Japan announces willingness to surrender to Allies, provided that the status of 124th Emperor Hirohito (1901 – 1989, Emperor for 63 years) remains unchanged • Allies refuse Japan's surrender offer to retain the Emperor Hirohito unchanged • Victory on Japan Day: Japan surrenders unconditionally • South Korea is liberated from the Japanese rule • Aisin-Gioro Puyi (1906 – 1967), the last Emperor of China (the twelfth and final ruler of the Quig dynasty) and ruler of Manchukuo, is captured by the Soviet troops • Indonesia (Dutch East Indies) declares independence from the Netherlands • At the proposal of the US President Truman, Korea is divided on the 38th parallel, with the US occupying the southern area, and the USSR the northern area • Russian troops occupy Harbin (northeast China, 1200 km northeast of Beijing) and Mukden (now Shenyang, northeast China, 600 km northeast of Beijing, and 600 km southwest of Harbin) • the Vietnam conflict begins as Ho Chi Minh (1890 – 1969) leads a successful coup • British troops liberate Hong Kong (southern coast of China, at the South China Sea, 2000 km south of Beijing) from Japan • General MacArthur (1880 – 1964) is named the Supreme Commander of the Allied Powers in Japan • the formal surrender of Japan takes place aboard USS Missouri, and the World War II ends • the first "bug" in a computer was discovered, a moth was removed with tweezers from a relay and taped into the log • Kim Il Sung (1912 – 1994) arrives in harbor of Wonsan, port of North Korea, on the westernmost shore of the Sea of Japan, 150 km east of Pyongyang • German rocket engineers begin work in the US • The US President Harry Truman announces that the atomic bomb secret was shared with Britain and Canada • the Chinese civil war begins, between Chiang Kai-Shek (1887 – 1975) and Mao Tse-Tung (1893 – 1976) • Juan Peron (1895 – 1974) becomes dictator of Argentina •

Germany 21 March 1978, Dortmund, Die Stoberecke (center right).

20 April 1978, Italy, Milano, the façade of il Duomo (1386-1965 (579 years), capacity 40,000, length 158.5 m, width 92 m, maximum height 108 m, 135 spires.

Japanese troops surrender Taiwan to General Chiang Kai-Shek • General Enver Hoxha (1908 – 1985) becomes leader of Albania for 40 years • UNESCO is founded • General George C Marshall (1880 – 1959) is named special US envoy to China • Yugoslavian Socialist Republic is proclaimed • the microwave oven is patented in the US • the Austrian Republic is re-established

Newton's quote: *Men build too many walls and not enough bridges.*

1946 Vrănceanu was elected to the Romanian Academy as a corresponding member.

First meeting of United Nations General Assembly opens in London (Jan.10) • Winston Churchill's "Iron Curtain" speech warns of Soviet expansion. The Cold War begins. • The first automatic electronic digital computer, ENIAC, is dedicated at the University of Pennsylvania. • The US Army makes radar contact with the Moon (400,000 km away) for the first time.

1947 Arciniegas, 47, felt that he and his family (including daughter Gabriela Mercedes) were in danger, and moved to the United States, taking advantage of an offer to teach at Columbia University. He lived in New York for ten years (1947–1957). Professor at Columbia University from 1954 until 1959.

Solzhenitsyn, 29, begins using a post as a school teacher of mathematics and physics, inside the scientific labor camps in Russia, as a cover to write. "The First Circle" would later chronicle this time period.

February 10: peace treaties for Italy, Romania, Bulgaria, Hungary, and Finland are signed in Paris. • On March 12 the Truman Doctrine proposes "containment" of communist expansion. • In June the Marshall Plan is proposed to help European nations recover economically from World War II.

Italy, 25 Jan. 1978, Vale d'Aosta, Pallésieux (1108 m) straight, Courmayeur (1224 m) and tunnel under Monte Bianco to right, Monte Bianco center up (Mont Blanc, 4,808 m, in France, Graian Apls, between the regions of Aosta Valley, Italy, and Savoie and Haute-Savoie, France; very close to Italy, the highest mountain in the Alps, and the highest in Europe west of Caucasus peaks, 11th in the world in topographic prominence), 15 km to the northwest.

1948   Gheorghe Vrănceanu was appointed Head of the Geometry and Topology department at the Faculty of Mathematics.

At the end of February, Communists seize power in Czechoslovakia. •   Edwin Land (1909 – 1991, US) invents the Polaroid Land camera.

1950 Solzhenitsyn, 32, is transferred to a labor camp for political prisoners in Russia, where he contracts stomach cancer. It clears in 1954, at 36, after treatment. The ordeal is later published as "The Cancer Ward" and "The Right Hand".
The Korean War began on June 25, 1950, when North Korean forces, backed by the Soviet Union and China, invaded South Korea.

1952   Arciniegas published the book *Entre la Libertad y el Miedo* (Between Freedom and Fear), often banned. The book analyzes a critical period in Latin-America, when seven dictators were in power in seven countries, at the same time. The publication and translation of the book was prohibited in at least ten countries. General Gustavo Rojas Pinilla, the President of Colombia, accused Arciniegas of being anti-Colombia, and ordered all of his books to be burnt. Rafael Trujillo, the dictator of the Dominican Republic, put Arciniegas on his hit list.

Plato's quote: *The penalty that good men pay for not being interested in politics is to be governed by men worse than themselves.*

27 March 1978, Bulle, 771 m, Switzerland, 40 km northeast of Lausanne, 30 km south of Fribourg, 3 km west of Lac de la Gruyère.

8 April 1978, Pisa, near Scuola Normale Superiore, 1810, by Napoleon Bonaparte (1769-1821), on the balcony of a private house.

Chapter 7. Academician Vranceanu, Ambassador Arciniegas

1953 The 34th U. S. President was Dwight D. Eisenhower: 1953-1961, 1890-1969 (78), Supreme Allied Commander Europe.

Solzhenitsyn, 35, after serving his eight-year prison term, receives a new sentence: imprisonment for life. Stalin dies on March 5, at 74, after 30 years of dictatorship. On September 7 Nikita Khrushchev (1894 – 1971) takes power in the Soviet Union and starts some reforms.

On July 27, 1953, North Korea, China, and the United Nations signed an armistice suspending all hostilities of the Korean War.

1955 Vrănceanu was elected to the Romanian Academy as a full member.

1956 Solzhenitsyn, 38, is granted a reprieve from incarceration. He becomes a mathematics and science teacher in Russia.

1959 Arciniegas was Ambassador of Colombia in Italy until 1962.

1961 The 35th U. S. President was John F. Kennedy: 1961-1963, 1917-1963 (46), U.S. Senator from Massachusetts.

Solzhenitsyn, 43, has his manuscript "One Day in the Life of Ivan Denisovich" (about a labor camp inmate) at "Novy Mir" editor Aleksandr Tvardovsky (1910 – 1971, Russian poet and writer). Tvardovsky supports the novel, publishing it in 1962, with the consent of Khrushchev, in a brief period of de-Stalinization. 27 years would pass before the Soviet Union publishes a second Solzhenitsyn novel (in 1989).

1962 Arciniegas received Order of Merit of the Italian Republic. He then was named Ambassador of Colombia in Israel.

1963 The 36th U. S. President was Lyndon B. Johnson: 1963-1969, 1908-1973 (64), 37th Vice President of the U.S.

June 1978, Verona (300 BC, municipium in 49 BC, elevation 59 m, population 269,000, area 206 km^2, on the river Adige, three of Shakespeare's (1564-1616) plays are set here), Piazza dei Signori, looking northwest to the statue of Dante Alighieri (1265 – 1321, poet (Divina Commedia (1308-1320), the Father of the Italian language, and one of the greatest poets of world literature), statesman, language theorist), Loggia del Consiglio (back).

1964 Vrănceanu was elected President of the Mathematics Section of the Romanian Academy.

Solzhenitsyn, 46, as Khrushchev is ousted, has his plays halted, and his unpublished novel "The First Circle" is seized.

1967 Arciniegas was Ambassador of Colombia in Venezuela until 1970.

1968 Solzhenitsyn, 50, completes his masterwork, "The Gulag Archipelago", a history of the labor camps in which he served. The book would become a powerful indictment of Russian dictator Joseph Stalin, who used the camps to hold political prisoners, in an attempt to destroy the opposition to the Soviet totalitarian state.

1969 The 37th U. S. President was Richard Nixon: 1969-1974, 1913-1994 (81), 36th Vice President of the U.S.

1970 Gheorghe Vrănceanu retired. During his career, Vrânceanu published over 300 articles in journals throughout the world. His work covers a whole range of modern geometry, from the classical theory of surfaces, to the notion of non-holonomic spaces, which he discovered.

Solzhenitsyn, 52, wins the Nobel Prize for Literature (before the publication of "Gulag"), but the Soviet state protests, preventing him from receiving the prize for years. His unpublished manuscripts begin leaking to the West, and Solzhenitsyn's literary fame grows.

1973 Solzhenitsyn, 55, has the first of the three volumes of "The Gulag Archipelago" published in the west. Alexei Kosygin's (1904 – 1980) Soviet government does not take immediate action. Also Solzhenitsyn marries his second wife, Natalia Svetlova. They have three sons: Yermolai, Stepan and Ignat.

USA, July 1980, from the New York Harbor looking northwest to New York City, and the southeast sides of the twin towers (1973-2001, first, with antenna spire (left), 417 m and second (right) 415 m, the square base for each was 63 m on each side, the core of each tower was 27 m by 41 m, with 47 steel columns). They were part of the World Trade Center (complex of 7 buildings in Lower Manhattan, on 16 acres, with 1.2 M m² of office space, 95 elevators).

Switzerland, 23 April 1978, Zürich (elevation 392 m – 871 m), population 400,000, on Limmat River, at the north of Zürichsee (Lake Zürich), in Bahnhofplatz. In Roman times, Turicum was a tax-collecting point at the border of Gallia Belgica (from 90 Germania Superior) and Raetia, for goods trafficked on the river Limmat. After Emperor Constantine's (272-337) reforms in 318, the border between Gaul and Italy was located east of Turicum.

1974 The 38th U. S. President was Gerald Ford: 1974-1977, 1913-2006 (93), 40th Vice President of the U.S.

Solzhenitsyn, 56, is labeled a traitor by the Soviet state-run newspaper "Pravda". He is stripped of his citizenship, and deported to West Germany. Solzhenitsyn lives in Switzerland, then continues his exile in Cavendish, Vermont, USA (160 km northwest of Boston), where he completes "The Red Wheel," a series of novels about the formation of the modern Soviet Union.

1976 Arciniegas was Ambassador of Colombia to the Holy See until 1978..

1977 The 39th U. S. President was Jimmy Carter: 1977-1981, born 1924, 76th Governor of Georgia.

1978 I met Ambassador Arciniegas and his family in Rome, Italy – he was an outstanding personality, distinguished intellectual, who made remarkable contributions to the progress of our culture and civilization. He gave us a real luculliano dinner (luculliano means "most generous", or "luxurious and lavish" in reference to a meal, and comes from Lucius Licinius Lucullus (118 BC – 56 BC, (62) a Roman politician in the late Roman Republic (connected with Lucius Cornelius Sulla (139 BC – 78 BC (61))), known for his sumptuous banquets).

11 Sept 1977, Roma, Lido dei Pini di Ardea (43 km south of Rome), second from left Germán Arciniegas (1900-1999, Colombian professor, historian, author and Ambassador to the Holy See)

1979 Professor Arciniegas was Dean of the Faculty of Philosophy and Letters at the University of the Andes in Bogotá, Colombia until 1981.

On April 27 Acad. Professor Gheorghe Vrănceanu, 2 months and 3 days before his 79th birthday, passed away in Bucharest. His mathematical research and results influenced many mathematicians, including T. Y. Thomas, V. V. Wagner, K. Yano, M. Dediu, A. G. Walker, K. Nomizu, S. Kobayashi.

Germany (southwest), 1978, Oberwolfach (the district of Ortenau in Baden-Württemberg, elevation 323 m (270 m to 948 m), population 2,500, area 51 km^2, in the central Schwarzwald (Black Forest) on the river Wolf, a tributary of the Kinzig.): Academician Professor Dr. Gheorghe Vranceanu (right) and Dr. Michael Dediu at the entrance to the Mathematisches Forschungsinstitut Oberwolfach (Mathematical Research Institute of Oberwolfach, founded in 1944 by the German mathematician Wilhelm Süss (1895-1958)).

Solar eclipse in the U. S. - totality was visible in Washington, Oregon, Idaho, Montana, and North Dakota, as well as parts of Canada and Greenland.

1981   The 40th U. S. President was Ronald Reagan: 1981-1989, 1911-2004 (93), 33rd Governor of California

1989   The 41st U. S. President was George H. W. Bush: 1989-1993, born 1924, 43rd Vice President of the U.S.

1992   Professor Arciniegas, 92, was appointed in Colombia President of the *National Commission for the Celebration of the Five-Hundredeth Anniversary of the Discovery of America*. He was summarily dismissed by then the wife (36 years old) of the President of Colombia, who took over the commission herself; an action that generated much opposition and protest.

1994   Solzhenitsyn, 76, following the reinstatement of his citizenship in 1990, after the collapse of the U.S.S.R., returns home, settles near Moscow, where he would live the rest of his life.

1999   At almost 99, by now blind and deaf, he was still dictating his twice-monthly column. On November 30, just 6 days before his 99th birthday, Professor Germán Arciniegas passed away of pneumonia, in Bogotá, Colombia, leaving a monumental work as a historian, author (over 70 books), essayist (over 15,000 essays and articles), diplomat, professor, statesman, and journalist. Colombian President Andres Pastrana decreed three days of national mourning for Professor Arciniegas.

2001

USA, July 1980, from the New York Harbor looking north to New York City, and the twin towers (1973-2001, 417 m and 415 m).

USA, July 1980, from New York Harbor looking northeast to the southwest sides of the Statue of Liberty and twin towers (1973-2001, 417 m and 415 m, 3.3 km away).

2008 On August 3, at age 89 and 7 months, the great Russian writer Aleksandr Solzhenitsyn, who significantly contributed to the collapse of the totalitarianism in the USSR and Eastern Europe, passes in eternity.

2017 On September 18: Doctors can now predict the severity of a disease by measuring molecules. Now some history:
- 1964 years from the birth of Trajan (53-117), the 13th Emperor (98-117) of the Roman Empire, which attained its maximum territorial extent.
- 1921 years from the proclamation of Nerva (30-98), at the age of 66, as a Roman emperor (96-98).
- 1693 from the victory of Constantin the Great (272-337) in the Battle of Chrysopolis (324, southeast on the strait of Bosphorus), establishing Constantine's sole control (324-337) over the Roman Empire.

Chapter 8. Other photographs

20 Oct 1977, Venezia, Basilica di San Marco (left back, 1156 – 1173, last restored in 1514), Palazzo Ducale (center and right)

1 Jan 1978, Pisa, from the west part of Piazza del Duomo, looking east to Torre di Pisa (1372, 56 m, white-marble, right), Cattedrale di Pisa (1092, center, striped-marble), and Battistero di San Giovanni (1152-1363, left, renown acoustics).

18 Dec 1977, Lo Sportivo Bardonecchia (1312 m, population 3200), Abbigliamento tutto per lo sci, Guardia di Finanza, Soccorso alpino.

Italy, 16 Oct 1977, Bardonecchia (1312 m, population 3200, 90 km west of Torino, 100 km south of Mont Blanc (4808 m)).

3 Sept 1977, Roma, Lido dei Pini di Ardea, a small city 43 km south of Rome (founded 21 April 753 BC, over 2.8 M residents, 1,285 km^2, elevation 21 m, over 2,700 years of globally influential art, architecture and culture on display, one of the oldest continuously occupied sites, called Urbs Aeterna (The Eternal City) and Caput Mundi (Capital of the World), with the independent state of Vatican inside the city boundaries) 15 km northwest of Anzio, looking southwest to the Tyrrhenian Sea.

20 Oct 1977, Venezia, Fermata Ferrovia (left), Chiesa degli Scalzi (center), and Ponte degli Scalzi (left)

USA, July 1980, Lake Placid (elevation 550 m) in the New York State's Adirondack Mountains, real snow, 180 km north of Albany

18 May 1978, Station de ski du Schnepfenried, France, 3 km southwest of Sondernach, on street D27.1, 50 km west of Rhine.

Italy, 1 June 1978, Cortona, on the road to Il Palazzone, Villa Principesca Sev XVI, looking west to Camucia and Vale di Chiana.

Italy, June 1978, Roma, COLVMNA·TRAIANI (113), commemorates Roman emperor Trajan's (53-117) victory in the Dacian Wars, constructed by Apollodorus of Damascus.

Italy, June 1978, Pisa, Cattedrale di Pisa (1092, striped-marble), Torre di Pisa (August 1173-1372, 55.86 m on the low side, 56.67 m on the high side, white-marble, 296 steps, right up).

June 1978, Consorzio Lido dei Pini Lupetta (by the Tyrrhenian Sea, 43 km south of Rome), Salvataggio.

June 1978, Consorzio Lido dei Pini Lupetta, by the Tyrrhenian Sea.

July 1978, Italy, Roma (753 BC, one of the oldest occupied cities in Europe, called Roma Aeterna (The Eternal City) and Caput Mundi (Capital of the World)), a building with beautiful statues.

July 1978, Italy, Roma (753 BC) in Piazza del Popolo (1822): the churches Santa Maria in Montesanto (left, 1679), and Chiesa di Santa Maria dei Miracoli (right, 1597, Rainaldi, Bernini, Fontana).

Italy, July 1978, Roma, a classical villa near Piazza del Popolo

Italy, July 1978, Roma, the central upper part of the northwest façade of the Patriarcale Basilica di Santa Maria Maggiore (435).

Italy, 29 March 1978, Roma, Laghetto di Vila Borghese, Tempio di Esculapio (1786, Greek temple of Asclepius, center right).

29 March 1978, Italy, Rome (753 BC), Arcus Constantini (315, for Constantine I (born 272, emperor 306-337)),

6 April 1978, Pisa, Battistero di San Giovanni (1152-1363, 55 m high, 34 m diameter, marble, acoustics, panels Pisano (1220-1284).

Italy, 11 Feb 1978, looking southeast to Spiaggia (Beach) di Mondello and Tyrrhenian Sea, 10 km northwest of Palermo, Sicilia.

Italy, 25 Jan 1978, Aosta, Banco Valdostano, signs for Torino and Milano to the right, and to Courmayeur, S. Bernardo to the left.

Italy, 29 Jan 1978, near Castello di Rivoli (950, 1159, 400 m), signs for Susa (50 km to west) and Torino (10 km to east) to the left.

Italy, 26 Jan. 1978, Vale d'Aosta, Lavancher, Pallesieux straight (4 km), Courmayeur (7 km) and Monte Bianco (4,808 m) right (20 km).

Italy, 25 Jan. 1978, Vale d'Aosta in northwest Italy, bordered by France (west) and Switzerland (north), in the Western Alps.

Italy, 5 Jan. 1978, Susa, 50 km west of Torino, elevation 500 m, population 7,000, in 20 BC voluntarily part of the Roman Empire.

Italy, 25 Jan. 1978, Aosta (583 m), Piazza Emile Chanoux, Commune D'Aosta (Hotel de Ville, Municipio), statue of a soldier (center left).

Switzerland, 23 April 1978, Zürich (elevation 392 m – 871 m), population 400,000, Limmat River (right), near north of Zürichsee.

Switzerland, 23 April 1978, Zürich (elevation 392 m – 871 m), population 400,000, on Limmat River, at the north of Zürichsee (Lake Zürich), in Bahnhofplatz. In Roman times, Turicum was a tax-collecting point at the border of Gallia Belgica (from 90 Germania Superior) and Raetia, for goods trafficked on the river Limmat. After Emperor Constantine's (272-337) reforms in 318, the border between Gaul and Italy was located east of Turicum.

24 April 1978, Oberwolfach (elevation 270 to 948 m, Black Forest), Germany, at Mathematisches Forschungsinstitut Oberwolfach

29 March 1978, Trajan's Market (113 AD) was an ancient mall that housed 150 shops and offices, north of Trajan Forum (113 AD).

USA, Ohio, August 1979, Sandusky (1816, elevation 182 m, population 25,000), by Lake Erie, 85 km west of Cleveland

USA, Arizona, Tucson (1877, elevation 728 m, population 530,000), May 1979, (the author was invited at the University of Arizona (1885, academic staff 3,000, students 43,000)).

USA, Ohio, Sandusky (1816, elevation 182 m, population 25,000), by Lake Erie, 85 km west of Cleveland), August 1979, Cedar Point (3 km north of Sandusky, has an amusement park with rides (center up back), has one of the largest collections of roller coasters (16) in the world, has the second tallest roller coaster in the world).

USA, Dec 1986, New York City, 341 9th Ave (at W 30th St), United States Post Office, "Neither snow, nor rain, nor heat, nor gloom of night, stays these couriers from the swift completion of their appointed rounds".

British philosopher from the University of Oxford, John Randolph Lucas (right, born 1929) and M. Dediu, on November 3, 2006, at the International Conference "John Stuart Mill, 1806 – 2006".

Addendum: For future generations

It is an insult for all the people to name hurricanes with people's names. Millions of people have asked the government to stop this abusive and insulting use of people's names (instead of using numbers and letters, like 1709TX), but the bureaucrats do not care. Work hard to change this bad habit by 2019.

Let's not forget that the people, of all countries on this beautiful Earth, want peace and prosperity, not war and poverty. Young women want to marry young men, to have strong families, to have children, grandchildren and great-grandchildren, and all to be healthy and happy! Continuously work for this, until it will be accomplished by 2399.

www.ingramcontent.com/pod-product-compliance
Lightning Source LLC
Chambersburg PA
CBHW041614220426
43670CB00001B/10